Brief Coaching with Children and Young People

Brief Coaching with Children and Young People: A Solution Focused Approach is the first book of its type to describe the thinking and practice of Solution Focused coaching with these age groups.

The approach empowers young people to find their own solutions in the shortest possible time, focusing on where they want to get to rather than the details of the problem they are concerned about. The authors' emphasis on practical and straightforward techniques and materials will equip all those interested in working with and supporting young people and their families to help them achieve their hopes for the future. The book is illustrated with numerous examples from the coaching practice of the authors in different settings, with a particular emphasis on challenging cases. As a whole, it serves as a key resource for working with children and young people, and each chapter can be read as a separate topic. Downloadable resources are available online which enhance the practicality of the text.

Ratner and Yusuf have created a practical, jargon-free resource for all those who work with and support children, young people and their families. It will be invaluable for coaches, therapists and counsellors as well as anyone who interacts with children and young people, including social workers, teachers and mentors and foster parents.

Harvey Ratner is a co-founder of BRIEF, established in 1989 as a London-based independent training, coaching and therapy agency for the development of Solution Focused practice. He and his colleagues Evan George and Chris Iveson have taught the approach to over 70,000 people around the world. They are the authors of *Solution Focused Brief Therapy: 100 Key Points and Techniques* and *Brief Coaching: A Solution Focused Approach* (Routledge). He works with young people and families in schools and at BRIEF.

Denise Yusuf, with a background in social work and management, is a freelance coach and supervisor who has spent most of her career working with children, young people and families. She works in a number of schools running coaching programmes for primary and secondary school pupils, as well as coaching children and young people from youth organisations and charities across London, and in her private practice.

Additional resources for this title can be downloaded from
www.routledge.com/books/details/9780415855891

Brief Coaching with Children and Young People

A Solution Focused Approach

Harvey Ratner and
Denise Yusuf

Routledge
Taylor & Francis Group

LONDON AND NEW YORK

First published 2015
by Routledge
27 Church Road, Hove, East Sussex, BN3 2FA

and by Routledge
711 Third Avenue, New York, NY 10017

Routledge is an imprint of the Taylor & Francis Group, an informa business

British Library Cataloguing in Publication Data
A catalogue record for this book is available from the British Library

Library of Congress Cataloging in Publication Data
Ratner, Harvey.
Brief coaching with children and young people : a solution focused
approach / Harvey Ratner, Denise Yusuf. — 1 Edition.
pages cm
1. Personal coaching. 2. Counseling psychology. 3. Solution-focused
brief therapy. I. Yusuf, Denise. II. Title.
BF637.P36R38 2015
158.3083—dc23
2014024603

ISBN: 978-0-415-85588-4 (hbk)
ISBN: 978-0-415-85589-1 (pbk)
ISBN: 978-1-315-74368-4 (ebk)

Typeset in Times New Roman and Gill Sans
by Florence Production Ltd, Stoodleigh, Devon, UK

Printed and bound in Great Britain by
TJ International Ltd, Padstow, Cornwall

Contents

Preface

Denise has a background in social work and management and gained the Diploma in Solution Focused Practice from BRIEF and a Diploma with Distinction in Life Coaching from the Life Coaching Institute. She is a Certified Coach with the Life Coaching Institute and an Accredited Coach with the Association for Coaching. She currently works as a freelance coach in schools, the voluntary sector and in private practice. Harvey is also from a social work background and after working in an NHS family therapy clinic he established BRIEF with Evan George and Chris Iveson, an agency that specialises in the practice and teaching of the Solution Focused (SF) model (details of courses and further information about the SF approach can be found at its website www.brief.org.uk). In 2012 BRIEF published two books, both with Routledge: *Brief Coaching: A Solution Focused Approach* and *Solution Focused Brief therapy: 100 Key Points and Techniques*.

Our intention is that this book will be as practical as possible and to this end we have been extremely liberal with examples of actual client work taken from our own experience (and where possible from recordings made – with the permission of clients – of sessions), as we believe that seeing or at least reading about real work is one of the most effective ways of learning a new approach. We have altered the case reports where appropriate in order to safeguard the confidentiality of the clients concerned.

Given the way we have drawn on our own practice, we have divided up the case work in the chapters so that we could use the word 'I' rather than having to define who the coach was in every case, as follows:

Solution Focused Brief Coaching: Harvey
Children: Denise
Adolescents: Harvey
Parents: Harvey
Groupwork: Harvey
In the school: Denise
In different settings: Denise
Materials: Denise

Coaching is a growing field and this book is the first to thoroughly explore Solution Focused Brief Coaching (SFBC) in relation to young people. However, we regard the potential audience for this book as being anybody who works with young people, in whatever capacity. The chapters are distinct, in the sense that the reader can choose to read the book through from beginning to end or could go straight to the particular headings that most interest them. However, we strongly recommend that you start with the first chapter, in which we look at the theory and skills involved, although we take certain generic coaching skills for granted, such as empathy.

A basic point to bear in mind from the beginning is that SFBC is a stand-alone model. Using this approach is not the same as a general focus on solutions which could be said to be true of all coaching approaches (after all, what coach would say they are *not* looking for solutions?). SFBC is a methodology for enabling clients to explore the lives they want to lead and their resources in achieving them.

This book not only draws on our own work but also that of our colleagues at BRIEF, Evan George and Chris Iveson.

Chapter 1

Solution Focused Brief Coaching

Solution Focused Brief Coaching (SFBC) is a change-oriented approach that enables clients to find their own solutions in the shortest possible time. It is based on eliciting their preferred futures, their strengths and skills for achieving them, and building on what they are already doing that is working.

The story behind the Solution Focused (SF) approach begins in Milwaukee, at the Brief Family Therapy Center which was established in 1977 by the husband and wife team of Steve de Shazer and Insoo Kim Berg. They put together a creative team of therapists and researchers to try out different techniques and understandings of brief therapy, and by the mid-1980s they had established the foundation for a whole new approach which they called Solution Focused Brief Therapy.

Three discoveries made by the Milwaukee team stand out. Firstly, they found that asking clients to describe *in detail* a future when the problem will be solved is itself empowering of clients to make their own advances. The technique that they developed to enable clients to picture the future has become known as the Miracle Question:

- Suppose that one night, while you are asleep, there was a miracle and this problem was solved. How would you know? What would be different? How will your husband know without your saying a word to him about it?

(de Shazer 1988: 5)

de Shazer goes on to say that 'we have found this way of quickly looking into the future to be a most effective frame for helping clients set goals' (de Shazer op. cit.: 5), and in the earlier phase of the development of SF interviewing the notion of *goals* was a dominant theme.

de Shazer remarked that 'the phrasing of the question includes a radical distinction between problem and solution, which is a result of our noticing that the development of a solution is not necessarily related to the problems and complaints in any way' (de Shazer 1994: 95). Elsewhere, he commented on how this discovery had led them to switch their approach from one of 'problem solving' to that of 'solution development' (de Shazer 1988: 1).

They also made a second discovery, seemingly obvious to us today but revolutionary then, that for almost every problem there is an *exception*, a time that the client's problem is either less or non-existent. One team member's account of how this came about describes how 'one day someone said "Let's ask them what they *don't* want to change" . . . subsequently we found that by asking clients to focus on exceptions rather than the problem, improvement tended to occur' (Lipchik 2009: 51–2). They were able to show how successful this intervention was in promoting solution behaviour which was from the client's *own* repertoire of skills and resources; there was therefore no need to try to stop anything the client was doing or get them to do something new.

The focus on the future and on successes in the past linked logically with the third discovery, namely, the value of a progress rating scale (de Shazer 1994), where clients are asked to rate their progress towards their goals on a scale. Some practitioners use scales from 0 to 10, and others from 1 to 10; one of the authors of this text uses the one, while the other author uses the other.

- On a scale where 10 stands for 'this whole package, the day after the miracle, and 0 for when things were at their worst' (de Shazer 1994: 231), where would you say you are now? How come?

The client's answer opens up two possibilities, namely, an exploration of what the client has done to reach their number (the exceptions) and then a discussion of *steps* that they could take to move closer to their goals.

This simple and economical model – of exploring a future without the problem and looking for exceptions and achievements – remains the foundation block on which all the subsequent developments in the SF approach have been built.

Developments in Solution Focused practice: the contribution from BRIEF, London

In 1990 the members of BRIEF (then known as the Brief Therapy Practice) published the first UK text on the approach (George et al 1990). It was closely connected to the model that had been constructed in Milwaukee, but when the authors issued a second edition, nearly 10 years later, they were able to describe significant adaptations they had made (George et al 1999). The key shift concerned the opening of sessions. Instead of asking 'what brings you in today?' (de Shazer 1991: 133), which invites a statement of concerns and problems (which then leads logically to the Miracle Question in which the 'miracle' is said to have solved those problems), clients are asked the Best Hopes Question (George et al op. cit.: 13):

- What are your best hopes from coming here?

or alternatively

• How will you know coming here has been useful?

These questions can be seen as generating a *contract* between the coach and the client. The client is directed away from problems towards their hopes – which then leads directly into a focus on their 'preferred future' (Iveson 1994) for when they have achieved those hopes. The contract is kept vague and general to guard against limiting the range of possibilities for the client in future, a point that de Shazer made in a prescient observation at the end of the last book of which he was the sole author, that to contract for specific goals 'would constrain and limit the possibilities for change and limit the possibilities for the clients to invent or discover something that satisfies them as much as, or more, than what they imagined or wished for when they described their ideas about the morning after the miracle' (de Shazer 1994: 273). From our perspective, the coach maintains a live connection between the contract established in brief, general terms – such as 'getting back on track with my life' – and the preferred future explored in concrete, detailed terms such as 'when that's happening, what will you be doing tomorrow?'.

Over the ensuing years, members of BRIEF have continued to explore the ramifications of this change of direction, and have published two books that describe in detail their current approach, including a general introduction to SFBC (Iveson et al 2012; Ratner et al 2012).

The idea of 'achieving your preferred future' is significantly different from 'solving your problem'. 'Strictly speaking, it is a mistake to see the client's description of a preferred future as a 'solution'. More accurately, it is an alternative way of living in which the presenting issues have no significant part' (Ratner et al 2012: 93). In enabling the client to develop this way of living, the solution to their problem occurs as an outcome to the work; it is solved by the client without any direct intervention by the coach. The strict attention paid to the contract ensures that the conversation doesn't veer off into irrelevant 'positive' thinking disconnected to the reality of clients' lives.

Thus the client is asked a different form of the Miracle Question, in which the miracle enables the client's hopes to be achieved overnight, or use is made of what has come to be called simply the Tomorrow Question (Ratner et al op. cit.: 93–4):

• Suppose you achieved your best hopes overnight, what would you be doing tomorrow?

This shift also leads to some changes in the language used to describe SF techniques. The idea of 'exceptions', for example, is closely connected to the notion of problems, and this has led to the application of a new term, that of 'instances', to indicate those times when the client is seeing signs of their preferred future already happening:

- From this description of what you want to see yourself doing in future, what would you say you are already doing, even in very small ways?

Another development has been an emphasis on what *signs* clients will notice when moving forward in their lives. For example, the client is asked what would be the signs of having reached a point up on the progress scale as opposed to what *steps* they have to take to reach the next point. What the client actually does to move up their scale is left to them to discover; the important thing is that they have a notion of what will be different *when* they have moved up.

- What would be the signs that you had moved up one point on the scale? What would you be doing differently then?

- Where on this scale would you be happy to get to? Where would be 'good enough'?

Further techniques that have been found to be useful will be discussed during the course of the book. Here we will mention one in particular, namely, the technique of 'identity questions' (Ratner et al 2012: 155). Here the client is asked, usually after they have described a step they have taken (however small):

- What did it take for you to do that?
- What does that say about you as a person?
- What does it tell others about your skills and qualities?

Young people are in a state of almost continuous change and so are often re-evaluating themselves; these questions about 'the person you are and the person you want to be' can be enormously revealing to them.

Ending sessions

The earlier Milwaukee model attached considerable importance to the way that sessions were ended. After taking a short break to consider what feedback to give clients, they would start by complimenting clients on anything they had reported that seemed useful in enabling them to move forward in their lives. They would then make a suggestion of a homework task for the client to work on before the next session. Milwaukee publications give numerous examples of different tasks, ranging from the simplest, such as inviting the client to look out for signs of progress (including moving up their scale), to more complex ones involving asking the client 'to pretend and act as if the miracle had happened' (de Shazer 1991: 114) or to predict at night whether the next day would be a good or bad day (to see what could be learned from their prediction, not whether it was right or wrong).

It is our practice to make the feedback to the client as brief as possible. The important work is in the interview itself, and there are times when we finish sessions without any further comment other than to enquire as to whether the client would like to return for a further meeting, and if so, when. On some occasions we end with a brief summary of what we have learned from the client, with a few compliments about their hard work and their achievements, and the only 'task' we are likely to give is to suggest that they look out for signs of improvement.

The stages of a first session

Opening. Resource Talk (that is, problem-free talk) as a way of 'getting to know the client' as a person rather than a walking problem. This step can come after contracting, and in any case can be regarded as optional.

Contracting. What are the client's best hopes from the work?

Describing the preferred future. Using the Miracle Question or the Tomorrow Question to explore the client's preferred future for when their best hopes have been achieved.

Identifying instances of success that are already occurring. Direct enquiry about what the client is already managing to do, even in small ways, and/or using a scale to measure progress – where 10 = their preferred future, and 0 = the worst it's been – and exploring how progress has already been made: how they reached their number on the scale.

Exploration of small signs of further progress. For example, how the client will know they have moved one point up on their scale. We regard this stage as optional; in many situations it will be enough for the client to know what they have already achieved to enable them to work out, on their own, what to do next.

Ending. The coach offers a short summary of the client's hopes and achievements. Again, this is optional.

Follow-up sessions

If sufficient work has been done in the first session regarding the clients' preferred outcomes to the work, then the main job of the brief coach becomes that of following up on whatever progress has been made. It is important for the coach to remember to enquire about *all* possible changes that may have happened, not only those that were specified as important markers in the first session. Indeed, it may not even be useful to mention the outcomes that were previously described (unless the clients themselves talk about having made progress on something they had wanted at the outset, as often happens). To do that risks the coach engaging in a checking-up process – 'did you do X, Y or Z?' – and it also means that other changes, that can turn out to be invaluable developments, may go unnoticed.

We cannot know what developments in clients' lives will be most valuable to them: it is as if 'solutions' can come from any part of their day-to-day life.

The structure of follow-up sessions then becomes, in effect, the opposite of the first session, in the sense that instead of beginning with future-focused questions, the follow-up begins with the coach focusing on the past, asking 'what's been better?' and then exploring who has done what to move things forward since the last meeting. Later in the meeting the coach will return to a future focus by asking what would be signs of further progress.

- What's been better since we last met?
- What are you pleased to have noticed yourself doing?
- What are others pleased to have seen you do?
- What have been the effects of that progress on others?
- Where are you on the scale now? How come?
- What would be signs of moving a point further up the scale?

The work is completed when the client feels they have achieved what they wanted from the outset. In most cases, the client is able to accept reaching their 'good-enough' point on the scale rather than having to get all the way to 10.

In cases where there have been setbacks, the client is asked questions about how they have managed to keep going:

- Given how difficult things have been, how have you managed to cope? What have you done that's impressed others?
- How will you know you're back on track?

There is no need to re-contract with the client or go back over their preferred future. However, if something drastic has happened since the last meeting (such as a bereavement or permanent exclusion from school or accommodation in local authority care), then it may well be necessary to revisit the Best Hopes Question to clarify what the client is now hoping for, given their radically changed circumstances in life.

Clarifying the contract: the client's best hopes from the coaching

The reader will notice that, throughout this book, great emphasis is laid upon the importance of clarifying the client's 'best hopes' from the coaching. If the coach is able to get this 'right', then the work subsequently is more straightforward (although not necessarily easy!). The many case examples in the book will enable the reader to gauge the wide range of 'contracts' that can be achieved with clients, and the context of the work will also influence the choice of outcome or goal that is reasonable for the work. For example, a young person may say that they wish to find ways to control their temper. From the coach's point of view, this is fine as a *basis* for establishing a contract for the work; it is not the contract itself, as it is problem-focused – controlling temper is a means towards something else, and the coach needs to know what that something else is. So the coach will ask an extra question – 'What difference will that make to you, to be able to control your temper?' – and once the young person has given an outcome-oriented answer, *that* becomes the contract: for example, that they will be happy and will have better relationships with people. On the basis of this contract, the coach will then move on to work out with the young person what in detail their preferred future might be once they are happier. The SF work is therefore about exploring the *difference* having control will make to their life and relationships, and later exploring ways they already have of doing those things. It isn't about examining ways of controlling temper, as would typify a more problem-solving approach. It is as if useful methods of control will emerge as a by-product of achieving the other aims.

But what if the young person were to answer the Best Hopes Question with a wish for something that is very hard to achieve or is downright unrealistic? What if they said, for example, they wanted rehousing, and this was something that the coach felt powerless to help with? The coach could feel justified in explaining that this wasn't part of the remit for their job and to 'signpost' the young person on to another service. In other words, the coach would be thinking that they don't have a 'common project' (Korman 2004) with the client. But an opportunity may have been lost here. The young person might feel discarded and not follow through with a new referral.

Another way forward would be, as before, to treat the goal of rehousing as a means to an end and to ask the young person what difference it would make to their life if they *were* rehoused. The coach might worry that such a question invites unrealistic thinking on the part of a client who might have an uphill struggle to get rehoused. However, we would recommend that the coach set that fear to one side and persevere with briefly exploring what the outcome might be in their life from getting rehoused. Let's suppose that out of that discussion it emerged that the young person hoped that they would be happier, free from the difficulties they were encountering in their current accommodation, and able then to go to college (or work) and able to thrive in their studies (or work). Then the coach could invite them to consider that being happier and thriving would be signs of a good outcome to the work, rather than, or in addition to, getting rehoused. Of course, the coach may feel they should mention that they are themselves not in a position to do anything about housing, if their worry is that the child or young person would be misled into believing that.

This approach enables the young person to explore what they, in a sense, *really* want in their lives and doesn't prematurely close down the coaching process. A good example of this is provided by John Sharry, who distinguishes between possible responses a coach can make to a child who says they want their parents to get back together. The coach could say 'That may not be possible. You know your mum and dad are separated' and ask the child to come up with an alternative

. . . which, unsurprisingly, leads to the child, no doubt feeling unheard, saying 'don't know' and looking away. In the alternative pathway the coach accepts the initial wish and enquires as to what would be different *if* the parents got back together, and the child then talks about everybody being happier and being able to spend more time with their father. The coach then summarises the contract in *those* terms, and the child says 'yeah that's it' (Sharry 2007: 25).

Questions to elicit description, not information

The answers that SF coaches are seeking are of a different nature to those in problem-focused conversations. In the latter, the coach is asking particular questions in order to get specific kinds of answers that are regarded as *information* that the coach can then use in deciding what is best for the young person. In SFBC, the coach regards the information as only of use to the client (Ratner 2010): it is as if we are asking questions so that the *young person* can hear their own answers.

When young people are enabled to describe in detail how their lives will be different in future, this is not seen as information about them but simply a *description* of a possible future. Then, together with the descriptions of the instances of success already present in their lives, the coach can be confident that they can step back and wait to see what changes young people actually make. The reader will see that a constant feature of this book will be the emphasis on the coach finding useful questions to enable clients to forge a description for themselves of what things will look like (or have been like) in the clearest detail possible. In general, the coach will choose between 'zooming in' to a scenario to elicit a closer description, or 'zooming out' to get a panoramic view of what else the young person and others might be doing. The what/where/when/who/how form of open questions (that is, questions that cannot be answered with a single answer like 'yes' or 'no') is favoured wherever possible, as is the practice of trying at all times to ensure that each question follows the client's last response, thereby enhancing the focus on detail that is relevant to them. It is not uncommon for clients to revert to the problem at some points, speaking about what they *wouldn't* be doing or *didn't* do. The coach then asks the question (dubbed 'The Great Instead' in Ratner et al 2012: 70):

• What will you be doing instead? What will others see you doing instead?
• What did you do instead? What did others see you do?

The coach can then delve into the responses before proceeding to the most commonly asked question in SF practice: 'what else?'.

The SF coach will want to consider how to link specific actions in the context of immediate concern to the client into 'in-your-life' scenarios. For example, a child concerned about a tricky meeting at school will want to focus on how they handle that scenario, and questions such as 'How will you know you're at your best in the meeting?' or 'How will you know you're doing yourself justice?'

(Iveson et al 2012: 190) will be particularly pertinent to them. The SF coach will then aim to extend that description beyond the immediate context into the 'life' of the young person. For example, 'Let's say you've been at your best in the meeting, what difference will that make to you? What difference will that make to you and your parents?'. These questions enable them to think about things in both a narrow sense (being at their best in the meeting) and in the wider sense of the differences to their life.

Being curious . . . and not being pushy

In some coaching models there is an emphasis on ending sessions with an action plan, a to-do list that specifies the what/where/when of what clients have to do in order to achieve their goals. In the current SF approach, action planning is avoided as much as possible – unless the client has specifically requested that this be worked on. We are concerned that an action plan acts mainly to put pressure on young people and put them in a succeed-or-fail position. If, instead, the young person has been able to describe in detail potential ways forward, then these descriptions will enable them to make their own choices out in the real world. Even if they choose to do things very differently from what they described in the session, it is within *their* control. What has been described in the session should be viewed only as *possibilities* for change (de Shazer 1994: ibid.). The coach's job is to cooperate with the client's pathways to change and to respond with questions that convey trust in the client and confidence that they can actually achieve what they want. So if, for example, they hear the child say 'I'd get up early' they wouldn't immediately ask 'how would you do that?' but instead ask questions such as 'what would someone else notice about you then?'. The point of a follow-up session with a client is to examine what changes they did actually make, whether these are close to what they described previously or completely different. If the young person has said they would get up early and in subsequent sessions they are saying they haven't managed to do this, in brief coaching it is necessary to rethink where the work is going, checking if the goal is still important to them and discussing what might be important now to help them move on – which could include questions about 'how' they are going to get up early or might be about other things entirely.

The usefulness of 'other-person perspective' questions

A frequently used line of questioning, derived from family therapy (one of the roots of SFBC), is where the coach enquires as to what *significant others* would notice the client doing in future that would be signs to them of progress being made, as well as times these others have already noticed progress.

- Who will be the first to notice that you are at your best tomorrow? What will they notice you doing?

Such questions add an extra layer to the question of what the young person will notice about themselves, and indeed there is then the possibility of a still further layer: of focusing on the *effects* of these changes on the others observing and what will be different between the two (or more) people. Thus an interactional, relational component is elicited that is enormously useful to young people in thinking through the impact of changes on their family and social and other lives:

• Will your mother be pleased to see you getting up early? How will you know she's pleased? What effect will that have on you? What difference will that make to your relationship with her? What will your sister notice that's different? What effect will that have on her?

If the sun doesn't shine

Suppose an adolescent were to say that they would know that things would be better tomorrow 'because the sun would be shining'. The coach would begin by accepting this, and ask how this would be good for them, and what it would lead them to do differently. What is likely to emerge is a description of the young person at their best, which might, in itself, be sufficient to spur them on to make changes. But it would be reasonable for the coach also to ask 'If tomorrow, when you woke up, and you were at your best and the sun *wasn't* shining, what would you be doing that showed you were continuing to be at your best?'.

Young people often complain about the actions of others. A child might say that their day would start well if their sibling didn't shout at them and instead was behaving nicely. While it would be important to ask about what difference it would make to the child if that happened ('I would be happy'), the coach might want to consider the possibility that what they wanted might not in fact happen. Then they could ask the child 'if that didn't happen, and you noticed that you were still a bit happier, what else would tell you that this was a day going well for you?'. An adolescent might say that things would be better for them in school if a particular lesson wasn't 'boring'. They can be asked about what would be different for them if it wasn't boring, what they would do then and what the teacher would see them doing. One 12-year-old boy talked about how it would lead to him not distracting others by talking loudly and making jokes; asked what he would do instead he said he would get on with the work. Asked what he would do if others began to disrupt the class and tried to get him to join them in that, he said he would ignore them. Then I asked him: 'suppose tomorrow you were at your best and you had a lesson that turned out to be boring, what would you be pleased to notice about the way you were coping with that?'. He said he would try to continue to focus on his work; he would ensure that he wasn't sitting next to friends he gets into trouble with, and although he knew he wouldn't be able to go a whole hour in that situation without making jokes, he would leave it as late in the lesson as possible before starting to do that, and do it in a quiet way and stop when told to. I asked him what it would say about him if he achieved that, and he said it would mean he was becoming 'mature'. That, of course, led me to ask him questions about what *that* would mean, what others would notice about him, what his friends would be impressed with, and so forth.

There are coaching models that encourage coaches to explore with clients what might be the 'blocks' (or barriers, or restraints) to change – see, for example, the GROW model (Whitmore 1996). 'Much coaching has been unable to resist the fascination of focusing on the question "What is it that is stopping this person fulfilling their potential?"' (Iveson et al 2012: 6). Part of the reason for this fascination is that the client is often asking themselves the same sort of question: 'Why can't I just do this? What's stopping me?'. It has been said 'That is the nature of coaching: it addresses cause, not only symptom' (Whitmore 1996: 67). From an SF point of view, coaching does not need to be about either cause or symptom, and the urge to search out blocks to be overcome should be resisted as much as possible. In the above examples, we are not searching for blocks to change. We simply accept that when young people refer to changes that would be taking place *outside of themselves*, whether in other people or things (like the weather, or boring lessons, or the team they support winning the league), then it is reasonable to enquire how they would continue to be at their best even if those things didn't happen.

Social constructionism

One writer on SF has suggested that clients can be said to talk themselves into their problems, and that 'solution talk' helps them talk their way out of them (Miller 1997). Clearly, SF practice relies on a sense that words are powerful – that what a person *says* can make a significant difference to what they *do*.

This thinking is related to the philosophical practices known as social constructionism (Gergen 1999). Put simply, this is a view that emphasises the ways that people 'construct themselves' through language, and how the language they use is itself constructed socially and culturally. Most young people are subject to a mass of pressures and expectations from the adult world, leading to problems that, in their view, have nothing to do with them and because of which 'just talking' won't, they assume, make any difference. Naturally, there are occasions when the coach will have to acknowledge that certain harsh material conditions – such as homelessness, the obligation to attend school, and rules in the school or workplace – are not liable to be changed through any amount of talking. But the SF coach will be looking, wherever possible, to develop conversations that highlight young people's own resources and skills so that they are empowered to better their situations, however slightly. A focus on hopes and successes enables young people, on occasion, to view their material difficulties and the way they relate to them in a different way and actually make surprising changes for themselves.

Another example about how language is used relates to the inevitable question arising in work with young people: how do we get beyond the 'ready answer'? Some responses may seem rehearsed, as in 'I'll go to bed earlier to get more sleep and then I'll get up earlier so that I won't be late for school/college/work'. A useful question here is 'How would that be good for you?' or 'What difference would that make?' where the aim is to enable the client to move from the *action* ('go to bed earlier') to the *meaning* ('it's important to me to do well in education and I want to please my parents and I want to show I'm not stupid'). We now move closer to the personal element rather than the headline rule that could apply to any student. Whether this is what the young person actually believes, or whether it is a belief that is co-constructed in the conversation, is immaterial as long as it is useful.

A point about the word 'conversation'. The emphasis on language and words has led some to say that SF is an approach that is not interested in feelings and doesn't allow clients to express emotions. From the social constructionist perspective, feelings are a part of language. Feelings, beliefs and behaviours are all interwoven. Thus, feelings are not seen as separate 'things' that cause people to act in certain ways, even though it is part of common parlance to talk about feelings in exactly that way, as if the client does things because of 'overwhelming feelings' that they have to express or 'work through' in order to be free of. This is not to say that in SFBC the young person is never asked about feelings, it is just that the focus will be on the 'better' feelings that they will hope to have in future, and what the outward expression of those feelings – the actions, that is – would be. Which leads to the misunderstanding that SF is all about being positive . . .

Not positive, but constructive!

A typical misunderstanding of SF is that it is all about ignoring a client's problems and 'being positive'. Take the example of a young person upset because their friend is being nasty to them. Typically, a coach would say that they have to show them empathy, meaning that they should ask them 'How did it make you feel when they were horrible to you?' and to express their understanding of those feelings. If, at the other extreme, the coach were to ignore the painful experience being described and responded instead by saying 'Tell me about the times you're *not* upset', then it would be reasonable to argue that SF is all about being positive and ignoring anything painful. But this is not what is done in SF practice; all good practitioners of SF have taken to heart the advice of Bill O'Hanlon of keeping one foot in acknowledgement and the other foot in possibility (O'Hanlon & Beadle 1994). This means that the coach acknowledges the pain *before* doing anything else. While they are unlikely to ask about the pain itself, they won't ignore it either – instead, they would, after acknowledging how difficult things are, go on to ask typical SF questions. Examples of this procedure in different situations would be statements such as:

- I imagine it was very hard for you when they said that to you and I'm wondering how you coped with that?

- It was obviously very painful for you when that happened and I'm wondering what conclusions you have drawn about what's best for you in future with these people?
- I understand that you felt so angry with them that you felt like hitting them. What did you do to resist that urge?
- What does that say about you as a person that you managed not to hit them even when feeling so angry?
- I understand that you felt so angry with them that you hit them and now you're wondering what to do about this in future. What will tell you that you are resisting the urge to get into fights this week?
- I understand that you felt so bad about that that you cut yourself. Would you like to find different ways to deal with strong feelings when they arise?
- Part of you thinks 'what the hell, I'm not going to go to college', and another part thinks 'it would be good for my future to go'. What goes through your mind when you think it would be good to go to college?

Using SFBC alongside other approaches

SFBC is a stand-alone model. It does not need to be used alongside other approaches to be effective, nor can it be integrated with them. SF conversations are of a radically different nature from problem-focused approaches that, for example, prescribe the necessity of accessing the client's problem first, or believe that different techniques are needed for different categories of problem, or say that for a client to be able to solve their problems they 'need' first to tell their story, and so on.

A coach might choose to start off a piece of work by exploring the young person's history in order to clarify their various problems. They might then move into SF questioning, such as how the young person's life might be different when the problems are solved. We would suggest that here the coach has moved from one approach to another; they have not integrated them, although of course the client will most probably not know that there has been a switch.

A typical coaching practice is that of finishing meetings with drawing up an action plan for the client to work on before the next meeting. We are not suggesting that that is 'wrong' (and indeed the reader will find other books on SF practice where their authors believe this is a valid or even necessary part of SF itself). Our point is more pragmatic, in keeping with the 'brief' tradition of which SF is a part, that the less we need to do in our work, the better.

We have a similar attitude to the question of teaching techniques to young people. For example, some coaches will argue that they can teach a child how to calm themselves, to de-stress in meetings, classes and other places, or can teach them anger-management techniques. Such an approach is inconsistent with using the SF approach where we are working to ascertain the young person's *own* expertise. Even if the child asks for our advice, we are loathe to give it as we believe that they will more easily act on the advice they give themselves rather than anything that comes out of our mouths. Can SF work alongside giving the client advice? A school mentor once said to us 'You ask so many questions! It's so much easier just to tell them what to do'. Well, we find that it is easier to find questions that help a young person think for themselves rather than struggling to come up with an idea they haven't already heard before. But if we really believe we have an idea that would help the young person – which happens very rarely! – we might be prepared to share the thought. Insoo Kim Berg said in a presentation that she would say to a client 'You have probably heard this before, but I've been wondering if it would be useful for you to . . .' – which is as respectful as it's possible to be when imparting advice.

The degree to which a coach may be able to stay closely allied to one approach such as SFBC will be influenced by the setting they work in and the expectations the context has of them. In this book there are chapters devoted to working in settings in which coaching of young people commonly takes place, such as in schools. There are many SF publications that describe how the approach can be used with different populations and in different agencies. To take a few examples from the UK, John Henden has written about work on preventing suicide (Henden 2008) and Frederike Jacob about work on eating disorders (Jacob 2001). For those in health settings there is the work of Kidge Burns (2005), Rayya Ghul and colleagues (Duncan et al 2007) and Alasdair Macdonald (2011).

Using SFBC in different contexts and media

Coaching with young people takes place in all manner of places such as schools, youth clubs, youth offending teams, outdoor training centres and the coach's own practice. Chapter 7 provides examples of how the approach may be applied in different voluntary settings. What is also of interest in work with young people is the format of the work, the medium of communication, as young people today are growing up with a wide range of digital media. While we focus on face-to-face contact in this book, we believe that SFBC lends itself without difficulty to other modes of contact, such as email, phone and Skype. There are young people who, for very good reasons of their own, will not attend for formal appointments but are willing to engage in conversations on their mobile phones. We think that it is, ultimately, a matter of choice for the client, and if they will be happier doing the work on Skype then the coach should collaborate with that; only if it is becoming apparent that the work is not succeeding should the coach discuss alternative ways forward with the young person. In other words, the SF coach is not assuming in advance that face-to-face is the right way for every client. We discuss below the absence, in SFBC, of an assessment process. The same applies to the lack of attention to a young person's non-verbal behaviour: facial expressions are not interpreted as meaning anything in particular. A young person is perfectly capable of looking bored and even contemptuous of the coach to the extent that the coach will feel they are wasting their time . . . and then discover later that they did indeed make good use of the conversation.

Effectiveness

The evidence for the success of SF Brief Therapy is now well established – see, for example, the comprehensive overview by Gingerich and Peterson (2013). The evidence for its use as a *coaching* model is less well documented, partly because it is much newer than its psychotherapy counterpart. Anthony Grant and colleagues in Australia have published several research studies (for example, Grant 2012) into its use in coaching but there have been questions raised about the nature of the SF practice that was used in the studies (George 2012). Their results nevertheless provide us with every reason to be confident that, in time, the evidence for the effectiveness of SFBC will be shown to be on a par with its therapeutic partner.

When SF work appears to be stuck

What does any coach do when their approach (whichever it is) doesn't seem to be working? They can (1) get supervision that will help them develop their ideas, (2) change their approach to another, or (3) refer the client to someone else – and there is the question whether that other person could use the same approach that appeared to fail or use a different one, as the change of person may be the significant factor for the client, rather than the particular model.

It is well known that the key factor in successful work, from the client's point of view, is the nature of the relationship they have with their coach (Duncan et al 2010). The suggestion has been made that when the work is stuck, this can be taken to mean that *collaboration* has failed (Jefferies, personal communication). From the SF point of view, then, the issue for the coach is how to establish or re-establish collaboration. The simplest route to that is to go back to the beginning and ask the young person what they are now hoping for from the work. In other words, a stuck case can be seen as an indication that the coach has lost sight of what the child wants. It may be that they have changed what they want without even realising it. But it's the coach's job to work that out.

Brief coaching

SF coaching is not only effective, it is also *brief*. Consider this example:

The 2-minute coaching session

The situation was of a 14-year-old student who was already known to me and whom I passed one day in the corridor of the school. The young man was standing outside a classroom. I stopped and looked enquiringly at the student who said he'd been thrown out of the class for talking. I asked if it was likely that the teacher would let him back into the lesson and he said 'yes'. I asked him if he wanted to go back in and again he said 'yes'.

Coach: So when the teacher comes out, what's he going to see when he starts to talk to you about going back in the classroom?
Student: That I want to go back in.
Coach: OK. What else?
Student: I don't know.
Coach: Well, how will you be talking to him about going back?
Student: I'll be serious.
Coach: How will he know that?
Student: I'll tell him that I won't mess around anymore.
Coach: And how will you look when you tell him that?
Student: What do you mean?
Coach: Well, what will be the look on your face?
Student: I won't smile.
Coach: What will you look like instead?
Student: I'll have a serious look, and look him in the eyes.
Coach: Sounds good to me. Good luck!

As I started to move on down the corridor the teacher emerged from the classroom and began talking to the student. I was too far off to hear what was being said but within 30 seconds the two went together into the classroom.

Obviously this is very 'thin' as a full coaching session goes. It was focused exclusively on the matter at hand (going back into a lesson) and so there was no chance to amplify this into an in-your-life description we usually recommend. But it is the sort of extremely concise conversation that anybody working with a young person can engage in as part of a bigger project of work with that client. And it makes a difference!

'Brief' can refer to both the length of a session and to the overall number of sessions. The research indicates that SFBC is generally brief in the sense of requiring fewer than ten meetings – maybe as few as, on average, two to four (Shennan & Iveson 2011). However, it can also be applied over long periods of time, and can also be used 'little and often'. Most of those who work with young people know that it is sometimes difficult to engage them for more than a short period of time, and there will be those who will have read the above transcript and thought of some young people they know who wouldn't have lasted even 2 minutes! The task we as coaches have is always to adjust to the young person, and if they will benefit from frequent short change-focused conversations then that is obviously preferable to seeking to enforce the famous 50-minute hour on them (in fact, we find that 30 minutes is the maximum time necessary for the majority of young people).

Regarding ending the whole work, it is of course important to the SF *brief* coach to know that they are on track to finishing the work in the shortest possible time, and they may ask clients to use a scale where '10 = we're done here, and 0 = when we first met', to gauge progress towards the outcome. However, there is no knowing for certain when in fact 'we're done' as only rarely, in our experience, do clients report reaching 10. Most young people are happy to be given a further follow-up appointment which, if things are truly moving forward for them, they then either cancel or forget to turn up for. In some contexts, such as in school, young people often like the idea of having a 'catch-up' meeting in 6 to 8 weeks after the meeting in which they have said they think they're 'done'.

Coaching, counselling, therapy: a word about labels

Apart from sports coaching, there was a time when coaching was seen as an activity related fairly exclusively to management, business and the world of organisations, and therefore focused on performance; coaching was to be seen as a goal-directed, future-focused and time-limited activity. Increasingly, organisations are looking to coaches to help their workforce to be happier and more creative, and many employees seek help from coaches in relation to career development, gaining a better work–life balance, and dealing with workplace issues.

While the training of coaches draws to a greater or lesser extent from counselling and psychotherapy models, coaches have in the past taken pains to show how their work is different from that of counselling. They have suggested that the latter is 'deeper' by focusing on the past and the feelings people have experienced, and is for those who have 'serious' problems and are therefore likely to need longer term work. They might suggest that a client seeks more specialist help for specific problems, such as substance misuse issues, mental health problems, marital concerns, and so on. They might also suggest that certain clients, especially those who are 'highly functioning individuals' (Houghton 2013), will benefit the most from coaching. However, increasingly, many coaches, especially those with backgrounds in psychology, see a place in their work for some of this more in-depth exploration that looks at feelings and past events, and recently a new approach called – a touch humorously – 'couching', has been proposed to combine the two (Houghton op. cit.).

In recent years, the term 'coaching' has begun to be used in a range of other services, such as parent coaching, with the result that the lines between counselling and coaching continue to become ever more blurred. With the development of the title 'life coach' it has become harder still to make a claim for the distinctiveness of coaching.

In summary, as the range of coaching practice expands, the differences between coaching and counselling are constantly being debated . . . and eroded. With regard to SF practice, it is pertinent to say that there is no difference between what an SF coach and an SF counsellor actually do. The work is based on the client's hopes from it, the commission in other words, and there is little evidence that different problems require longer SF work to resolve them. Whether the SF practitioner calls himself/herself a coach or a counsellor is likely to be determined by the client or customer group to be worked with. With regard to work with young people, our experience has been that young people are often deterred by terms like 'counsellor' or, worse still, 'psychotherapist'. Using the term 'life coach' has, in our experience, been a kind of client-friendly term that causes no fear, even if, on occasion, it isn't immediately clear to a young person what it means!

Assessment

It is considered axiomatic in most counselling and therapy models, and often also in coaching, that an assessment of the client's presenting problems, and the 'real' problems underlying them, is the first requirement of the work. In many agencies, this is part of the 'intake' procedure, and is often related to the concern to identify safety concerns, as will be discussed shortly.

In SFBC there is no assessment procedure. For example, when a client calls BRIEF and says 'I have 'X'. Do you work with that?' the answer will always be 'yes', regardless of what 'X' is, because, as we have seen, the approach is focused on what the client wants in future, not what they are unhappy about. This is of course often perplexing to clients: from time to time someone will say 'How can you help me if you don't know what my problem is about?' to which the simplest reply is for the coach to say 'The evidence is that it *does* work, but there are no guarantees, and anyway you should feel free to tell me about anything you think might be important for me to know'.

It can also be frustrating to some professionals too. There are coaches in private practice who make initial assessments a standard feature of their work partly to pick up on 'risk' factors from the outset but also to weed out inappropriate referrals. For coaches working for an agency, if doing an assessment first is part of that agency's procedure, then it has to be done, whether the worker is SF or not. In such situations we advocate a sort of mental exercise, whereby the worker imagines that they are carrying out the assessment in one room (the 'assessment room', which may just exist in their mind), before putting the completed assessment form aside and moving into the 'change room' to begin the SF change work.

Where an assessment has to be carried out, the role of SFBC is severely limited as it has nothing to contribute as to the nature of problems and their definition. However, there is a place in many assessments for consideration of a client's goals from the work and their strengths and potential for change, and SF questions can be incorporated.

When safety is a concern

No discussion regarding work with young people would be complete without a consideration of what to do when there are – or appear to be – safety issues. It needs to be stated emphatically that, as protection comes before anything else, where the coach has reason to suspect that the safety of a young person (or of others) is being compromised, then they have a duty to respond to this, even though this may mean stepping away from using the SF approach.

For example, in a case in the school context, a year 8 (12-year-old) student with learning difficulties had said, in response to the Best Hopes Question, that 'it' would stop. I asked how that would make a difference to him and he said he'd be 'happy'. I continued to explore what would be different in his life if he were to be happier, thus sticking with the outcome-focused nature of preferred future interviewing. But the young man from time to time referred to 'when it stops', highlighting that there was something significant that was bothering him. I asked him what the 'it' was and he said he was being bullied. At this point I moved into assessment-style questioning, checking what was happening to the student, what he tried to do to help himself, and who he had spoken to. I therefore moved completely away from the client-led nature of SF work as I was now seeking specific information on which to base any action I might need to take. It took only a few minutes to establish that very little had been done to help him, and as the time for the session ran out I suggested that he go along with me to tell his tutor what was going on. He was at first reluctant. His biggest concern all along was that the bullies would find out he'd told people; at one point, when I asked if he'd thought of talking with the school's police officer, he said that he was afraid that if, say, he were to ask permission to leave the class and go to the toilet and then make his way to the policeman, that one of the bullies might have followed him down the corridor. This, of course, only increased my sense that something needed to be done, and soon, and I gave him the choice of going with me to see the tutor or leaving it to me to have the conversation. He agreed to an immediate meeting, and in time the matter was able to be resolved.

Where safety is an issue, whether from bullying, self-harm, substance misuse and so on, the coach has to make a decision as to whether he or she needs to refer on to someone who can deal more effectively with the situation. The question of when and how a coach decides this is probably worthy of a book all on its own. For one thing, a lot will depend on where the coach is seeing the young person and who they talk to about their work (supervisor, manager). Serious decisions should wherever possible be taken in conjunction with another colleague.

In another case, a 16-year-old young woman seen in the school said her best hopes were that her older brother would stop beating her. She described how she would tell her family she was going to bed at 5 p.m., just so that she could avoid the brother, and she'd stay in her room until it was time to go to school the next day. When I asked about what her mother had to say about the situation, she told me that her mother had told her not to tell anyone about it in case social workers came round. I told her that I agreed with her that it would be better for this intolerable situation to stop, and that I had a duty to inform the child protection manager in the school. The young woman asked me not to tell her, but I said I had no choice and that we could both talk to that teacher together or I could tell the teacher myself. She opted for both of us to talk to the teacher concerned who, after being called to the coaching office, said she had looked at the student's file first and had a sense of some family issues; after hearing the young woman talk about her difficulties with her brother, the teacher said that she would immediately contact social services. I then talked with the young woman about how she hoped best to handle this situation, given that her mother would be unhappy and the brother would soon learn what his sister had alleged, and how best she could be supported through this difficult time.

We could give many more examples where it has been necessary to discuss with young people the need to pass on information. Usually they come to accept this and maybe that is what they were hoping for from the start, but there have also been occasions when the student has been furious that confidentiality has been breached and has subsequently refused to meet with the coach. Of course, it is important for the coach to have established at the outset that confidentiality has its limits, but we have experienced some young people still expressing surprise when we say we have to pass on information. One furious young man said that yes, he remembered being told about confidentiality, 'but I thought that only applied if I said I'd killed someone!'.

Thinking . . . and doing

A young man of 14 said to me 'coaching should be positive, not to make them feel better, but engaging them to *do* better stuff'. We couldn't put it any better ourselves. But one just has to wait and see whether that 'engagement' *has* been effective. An 11-year-old boy, at the end of his first one-to-one session, said to his mother, when she joined us to round off, that he would be prepared to return for one more session but he wondered how it was supposed to help him. His mother patiently explained that 'it's good to talk' to which he responded 'yeah, but what are you going to *do*?'. I complimented him on his excellent question and reiterated some of the excellent ideas he'd expressed earlier to me and asked him to look out for what he did that worked . . . and if he didn't see anything, then we would know it hadn't worked and would have to think of something else. Which, thankfully, didn't prove necessary!

The last word goes to a 15-year-old boy who, at the start of the fourth session, told me that things were much better. I asked him what had made the difference for him and he said, 'You've helped me to think about what I do when I'm happy and how to apply that at other times. I couldn't have done that without these meetings'.

Summary

Key assumptions in SFBC

- Successful work depends upon the client defining for themselves what they hope to achieve from the work

- Clients are empowered to make changes when they can describe their preferred futures in detail

- Change arises from clients describing both their preferred futures and the achievements they have already been able to make (however small)

- It is not necessary for the coach to know the details of the problem – or even what it is – for clients to be able to benefit from the approach

- The coach acts as a catalyst to change by means of asking questions that require the client to reflect on themselves, rather than the coach gaining any understanding of the client's life or of what they think, in an expert way, might be good for the client to do or not to do

- Clients live their lives through relationships to significant others, and questions that relate to their preferences for those relationships enable them to make meaningful changes

- There have almost always been instances of success, however small, in the client's life. The client has the resources for change

Key techniques

- **Best hopes**: The client is asked at the outset what their best hopes are from the work and this provides the coach with a 'contract'

- **Preferred future**: The client is asked the Tomorrow Question or the Miracle Question to identify what their life would be like the next day after their hopes have been achieved

- **Scale**: Where on a scale of 0 to 10 is the client now? What are they doing and how did they achieve it? What would be signs they had reached +1 on the scale?

- **Ending**: Summary

- **Follow-up sessions**: Asking about and amplifying progress

References

Burns, K. (2005) *Focus on Solutions: A Health Professional's Guide*. London: Whurr.

de Shazer, S. (1985) *Keys to Solution in Brief Therapy*. New York: W.W. Norton.

de Shazer, S. (1988) *Clues: Investigating Solutions in Brief Therapy*. New York: W.W. Norton.

de Shazer, S. (1991) *Putting Difference to Work*. New York: W.W. Norton.

de Shazer, S. (1994) *Words Were Originally Magic*. New York: W.W. Norton.

Duncan, L., Ghul, R. and Mousley, S. (2007) *Creating Positive Futures: Solution Focused Recovery From Mental Distress*. London: BT Press.

Duncan, B.L., Miller, S.D., Wampold, B.F. and Hubble, M.A. (Eds) (2010) *The Heart and Soul of Change: Delivering What Works in Therapy*, 2nd ed. Washington: American Psychological Association.

George, E. (2012) Solution focused questions work better in coaching – Anthony Grant. Blog at http://www.brief.org.uk/blog/?p=127.

George, E., Iveson, C. and Ratner, H. (1990) *Problem to Solution: Brief Therapy with Individuals and Families*. London: BT Press.

George, E., Iveson, C. and Ratner, H. (1999) *Problem to Solution: Brief Therapy with Individuals and Families*, 2nd ed. London: BT Press.

Gergen, K.J. (1999) *An Invitation to Social Construction*. London: Sage.

Gingerich, W.J. and Peterson, L.T. (2013) Effectiveness of solution-focused brief therapy: a systematic qualitative review of controlled outcome studies. *Research on Social Work Practice* 23(3): 266–83. http://rsw.sagepub.com.

Grant, A.M. (2012) Making positive change: a randomized study comparing solution-focused vs. problem-focused coaching questions. *Journal of Systemic Therapies* 31(2): 21–35.

Henden, J. (2008) *Preventing Suicide: The Solution Focused Approach*. London: Wiley.

Houghton, S. (2013) Lying on the 'couch': where coaching and counselling meet. *Coaching Today* Jan 2013: 10–15.

Iveson, C. (1994) Preferred Futures – Exceptional Pasts. Presentation to the European Brief Therapy Association Conference, Stockholm.

Iveson, C., George, E. and Ratner, H. (2012) *Brief Coaching: A Solution Focused Approach*. London: Routledge.

Jacob, F. (2001) *Solution-Focused Recovery From Eating Distress*. London: BT Press.

Jefferies, Y. (2014) Personal communication to meeting of London SF Forum at BRIEF, 7 January.

Korman, H. (2004) *The Common Project*. Available at www.sikt.nu.

Lipchik, E. (2009) A solution focused journey. In Connie, E. & Metcalf, L. (Eds) *The Art of Solution Focused Therapy*. New York: Springer.

Macdonald, A. (2011) *Solution-Focused Therapy: Theory, Research and Practice*, 2nd ed. London: Sage.

Miller, G. (1997) *Becoming Miracle Workers: Language and Meaning in Brief Therapy*. San Francisco: Jossey-Bass.

O'Hanlon, B. and Beadle, S. (1994) *A Field Guide to PossibilityLand*. London: BT Press.

Ratner, H. (2010) Blog posted 12 September 2011 http://www.brief.org.uk/blog/?paged=4

Ratner, H., George, E. and Iveson, C. (2012) *Solution Focused Brief Therapy: 100 Key Points & Techniques*. London: Routledge.

Sharry, J. (2007) *Solution-Focused Groupwork*, 2nd ed. London: Sage.

Shennan, G. and Iveson, C. (2011) From solution to description: practice and research in tandem. In Franklin, C., Trepper, T.S., Gingerich, W.J. and McCollum, E.E. (Eds) *Solution-Focused Brief Therapy: A Handbook of Evidence-based Practice*. New York: Oxford University Press.

Whitmore, J. (1996) *Coaching for Performance*, 2nd ed. London: Nicholas Brearley.

Chapter 2

Children

Why coach children?

Children may see a coach for a variety of reasons. It may be that parents or other adults in the child's life have concerns about how the child is managing, and seek help, or perhaps it's the child who has worries or is experiencing difficulties. Many difficulties get resolved during the normal everyday life of the child, with the help of friends, family, teachers and other adults known to the child. However, sometimes children will go on worrying or behaving in a way that stops them from getting on with their lives – for example, seeing themselves in a negative way, struggling to manage their behaviour, or not being able to achieve in their work. Solution Focused Brief Coaching (SFBC) can be an effective way to help children find their voice, express themselves, and find their own solutions.

Solution Focused (SF) coaches can work with children on their own or as part of a family group, depending on what would be useful or what the client or referring agency requests. Confidentiality issues always have to be considered, but SFBC can be advantageous here in that it lends itself more easily to transparency. Children are often happy to tell parents or have someone else tell parents what happens in a session, and adults can feel the same, perhaps because of the strengths-based and future-focused nature of the conversations.

There may be times when the SF coach has to move into a different role when working with children. For example, if there is a possibility that a child is unsafe, then the coach needs to move out of the coaching role in order to do a risk assessment, or to refer on to the appropriate professional who can do this. If there are problems with other people which need to be addressed – for example, bullying by another child, or a problem with another adult – then the coach may move out of the coaching role to deal with this, usually with the child's consent and contribution. And in working with children, many professionals may find themselves facing complex structural issues which can, and do, distress and disempower children as much as they do adults – for example, challenging social or financial hardships. It is important for practitioners to be aware of these complex issues as they impact on a child, and at times the SF coach may choose to move out of their coaching role to address these issues; at other times they will acknowledge them to the child and work to help the child to manage them. Deciding on which path to take could, in itself, be seen as a political as well as a professional practice decision. Making decisions about these issues as a professional can involve thinking about the impact of coaching not just on the child but on the wider environment.

Why use SFBC with children?

Children do not generally respond well to conversations in which 'problem talk' is dominant. Their sense of time means that what happened yesterday and what is going to happen tomorrow is more important than a problem which may be ongoing but not happening for them that day. In addition, talking about problems is often a very uncomfortable and restrictive experience for them. On the other hand, talking about strengths and resources, about the future, and about small successes, is a different way of talking, which also, as Therese Steiner says, connects with how children think and see the world:

> After all the solution focused approach fits very well with the way children think about and view the world. I have never met a child who liked to talk about problems. When you observe small children, how they solve little everyday problems goes along the predictable pattern of trial and error. They always look ahead, and they almost never sit down and analyse the difficulties in order to come up with a solution. The longer I thought about these characteristics, the more it became clear to me that SFBT [SF Brief Therapy] paralleled a child's way of being in the world.
>
> (Berg and Steiner 2003: xv)

SFBC sees the person as the person and the problem as the problem, and seeks to communicate with the person aside from their problems. This immediately expands the person's horizons so that they see more of their personal problem-free landscape, and it gives a sense of hope and energy from the very beginning of the work. This perception is particularly useful with children, because they are still developing their sense of identity, and whilst this ongoing development can give mobility and flexibility, it can also make children very susceptible to self-labelling. Problem-free conversation reminds the child that there is much more to them than their problem or worry.

SFBC can start to build for children a sense of self efficacy. They are able to talk about what they want to do differently, discover that they are doing some of this already, start to take small steps towards doing more, and move on from periods where no change happens or things get worse, all of which helps them to experience a sense of autonomy and agency. This often generates positive feelings and optimism about other things they might want to do differently and a sense of resilience about dealing with setbacks, which inevitably occur. This is really important to learn and experience early on in life and can lead to achievement in all aspects of a child's life.

Coaching can be particularly empowering for children because inevitably their environment is often controlled by others. SFBC helps children to understand that not only does change happen in other people, or in the environment, but that they can also do something different themselves. For example, a child who says that no one will be friends with them can discover their friendship-making skills which will help other children to be friendly towards them.

All coaching models contain assumptions that steer the process and progress of the work. The assumptions in SFBC are particularly child-friendly and position the coach in a different place, not leading the child to water but following the child to their own oasis.

What does a coaching session with children look like?

Just talking, not painting

I had recently started a coaching programme in a school and was talking in the staff room with one of the Teaching Assistants. This is how the conversation went:

'I think it's really great what you are doing with the children.'

'Oh good, I'm glad', I responded. 'What do you like about it?'

'Well, they love rolling up their sleeves and getting their hands dirty and they like being creative ... they don't get enough of this nowadays, so they love coming for their sessions with you.'

'Er, what do you think I am doing with them?' I asked tentatively, wondering if strength cards and stickers were a metaphoric rolling up of sleeves.

'Well, aren't you painting with them, I thought you were giving painting classes?' she said quite loudly, as the talk in the staff room ebbed. She was already starting to look a little disappointed.

'Well, not exactly, they are being creative but more with their own words and ways of looking at things, we are looking at their strengths and things they are good at and then what they want to get better at, pictures of how that would look, signs of them getting there ... painting with their words really ... that sort of thing ...'

'Oh', she said. 'Just talking then.'

The essence of an SFBC session is a conversation, and children (as opposed to teenagers) are usually happy to have a conversation. They are also familiar with the idea of a coach – although an SF coach might be a bit different from their expectations. Children are often used to viewing a coach as someone who can teach them particular skills as well as help them develop their talents, so it can be a welcome surprise to find that an SF coach is not going to tell them what to do or how to do it. Children also enjoy talking more when they are not being pushed to either talk about something they don't want to talk about or to give a particular answer. Resource-based conversations are easy ways to start talking with children, and enquiries about what children like doing, what they are good at, what their talents are, and what they have been enjoying recently are often positively experienced by children, who may have less inhibition than teenagers in answering these questions. Their answers will provide a wealth of riches to be drawn on later in the session.

In order to support and extend the conversation, the SF coach can introduce materials and activities such as role play, drawing, play, and other aids to communication. Children often enjoy using different materials and activities to communicate and express themselves. They may be used to doing this, or it may be that they don't get enough opportunities, so it should not be a challenge to introduce these into your sessions to help children to express their wishes and hopes, their strengths and skills, their achievements and their progress. It is important to ensure that any materials and activities are used as an integral part of the SF coaching process and not just stand-alone activities, interesting though these may be. Materials can be as simple as pens, crayons, paints and blank paper or card. They can be predesigned sheets and pictures for the child to complete. They can be particular SF resources such as 'strength cards' (St Lukes Innovative Resources www.innovativeresources.org), which are cards with different strengths and qualities written or illustrated on each card, coaching cards, record cards and pictures of scales; and they could be toys, soft toys and the environment around the child (see Chapter 8). In some sessions it can be helpful to use materials and activities, and in other sessions an SFBC conversation will work well enough without the need to introduce anything else. It is useful to be clear about what you are doing with other professionals, however, to avoid misunderstandings and disappoinments!

Sometimes, when using materials with a child, your physical positioning can have advantages. Some children can find sessions easier to manage – and less demanding or even less intimidating – if you are sitting side by side with them and looking at something together. This means that they can be in control of how much eye contact they wish to make, and 'thinking time' can be more relaxed.

It can be useful for some children to incorporate some activity into a session because they may find sitting difficult, or just less engaging. Even simple activities around the SFBC conversation, such as getting up to draw a scale on a board, or pointing to numbers on a big scale on the wall or floor, can be a good idea. Inviting the child to sit in different chairs when thinking what other people in his/her life might be pleased to notice or have noticed can also work well. Selekman (1997) has described many SF art activities and play exercises which I have found very useful in working with children – and, indeed, some adolescents too. Selekman describes these as part of Family Play, and I have found them to work equally well with children on their own in sessions. The following are some examples:

1   The imaginary-feelings X-ray machine. The child lies on the floor and has someone draw their outline. Then they write or draw inside the line all the feelings that the machine might show up, perhaps circling the ones they want to see more of.

2   Visualising movies of success. The child constructs an internal movie of a past success to use as a guide for a future success.

3   The Time Machine. This can also be drawn – or made in the room from chairs. The child can be invited to go back to a place in the past where things worked better, or forward to a place in the future where they would like to be. This offers lots of opportunities for the child to be talking about past successes, and they can look back from the future place (where their 'best hopes' have been achieved) to give themselves advice along the journey or notice how they are moving forward.

4   The Famous Guest and the Stuffed Animal Team. Children can be invited to think about famous people, past or present, or famous characters whom they admire. Children usually find this very easy to do, whether it is a footballer, a music or TV star, or a fictionalised character. They are then asked to think what this person might advise or suggest or notice about what they are trying to do to improve things; it usually works best if the child draws or finds a picture of the Guest, or stands in a special part of the room to represent the Guest, and it can produce a lot of laughter as well as some really good observations. For younger children it can be useful to ask them if they have favourite stuffed toys. The child can then be invited to ask this Stuffed Animal Team for their advice on how to handle things or what they have noticed the child is doing well.

Therese Steiner also describes wonderful ways of working with younger children using hand puppets, usually in the form of animals, where the practitioner talks to the hand puppet and the child answers in this role, 'at a safe distance from themselves, while at the same time experiencing parts of their own behaviour or the behaviour they will strive for in the future' (Berg and Steiner 2003: 78).

It is important for the SF coach to beware of adding anything to the observations produced by these activities. The ideas are solely the child's, and the activities are just ways of helping the child to generate more ideas, observations, and thoughts of their own.

An example of a child being helped by the image of a third party in the room concerns a 10-year-old child, Zoe, although her drawing represented a real animal, her dog Bunty, and not a stuffed one. Zoe wanted to be calmer and more relaxed. I asked Zoe what she would be doing then, and she described how she would talk more slowly, make her voice smaller, be able to stay in class and be quiet at home sometimes and listen to her mum and dad for a bit longer before jumping in (interrupting). The 'person' who would notice this most according to Zoe (with good reason it seemed) was Bunty. Bunty was a nervous and excitable young dog and used to get very upset if Zoe started getting angry and shouting. She would either hide under the table, or jump about barking non-stop. Zoe drew a picture of Bunty, and spoke for her, which of course included a lot of growls and woofing noises. Bunty turned out to have great observational powers at home and at school, and was always able to see that extra detail of calm behaviour that Zoe might have missed. Zoe carried round the picture of Bunty with her, and much progress was made, with Bunty seeing more and more change in Zoe, and Zoe beginning to see some change in Bunty. By the end of the sessions Zoe reported that Bunty had stopped barking and hiding under tables and was busy instead playing with Zoe, who had more time to play with her, because she spent less time shouting and getting angry. Zoe was also staying in class.

Role plays can be very effective SF activities, and some children will be able to show you how things are and how they want them to be, as well as what's been better, by acting them out with you in a session. Role play is particularly useful because it demonstrates the concrete observable actions that SF coaches are interested in, and the child might find it easier to act these out as a precursor to describing them. One girl, who could not move around the school freely because she felt that other children standing in groups were talking about her, showed me how she wanted to be able to walk about the school, with her head up, sometimes smiling, sometimes making eye contact, and even going up to people to talk rather than waiting for them to come to her. During this demonstration she noticed that she was already behaving like this in some small ways. My questions about what else she was doing, and what this told her about herself, added breadth and depth to what could have been a single unconnected description. I have also used role play in sessions very effectively when working with children who have friendship issues. The child can role play himself or herself, and the coach can role play possible friends; roles can be swopped, with feedback given – for example, the 'friends' can give good feedback to the child about what is working. The coach will often notice that the child has already done some of these things before, and sometimes the child will notice and say: 'I did that last week!'. However, some children do not seem to find role play appealing, and for them, other strategies, or simply conversations, work better.

For children who come into the room with a lot of energy it can be useful, if it is possible, to take an 'SF walk' outside. For this I am grateful to Peter Szabo who once sent all the participants on one of his courses in London out to do an 'SF walk' in Regent's Park (Szabo 2006). It was not only for fresh air and exercise (though this was welcome), but so that we could utilise trees, bushes, walls, statues, and winding paths as part of our SF conversations. We returned tired and inspired, having completed some very effective SF interviews with our partners! In a similar way an 'SF walk' with a child can include steps, jumps, or just particular natural phenomena, such as a big tree, to symbolise the child's skills and strengths. The sky, or other natural vista, can be focused on as the child describes 'best hopes';

collections of stones or twigs or leaves can be made for each detail of the preferred future; and paths, tree branches, hills or hedgerows in the natural environment can be utilised as scales, with the advantage that the child can run or walk these scales to show achievements so far and possible future signs of progress. These are just some ideas and you will find many more opportunities yourself in the outside world with a child. I have also incorporated some simple mindfulness exercises into the beginning of sessions. This is not to dissipate or decrease the energy in the room but to help the child to focus their energy. We sit quietly for a few moments, focusing our attention on being calm and on doing one activity such as breathing or getting up and sitting down very slowly and with great concentration.

Solution Focused skills and techniques with children

Starting the conversation

Starting sessions with children can often feel more comfortable for them if the conversation begins with a little general talking and expressions of interest in them, if only because they may have some fears or odd ideas about what sort of person or practitioner you are. As well as dispelling myths and fears, some general chat and questions can be experienced as more polite in some cultures, shows that you see the person as more than any problem, and is an opportunity for the child or

---

Finding strengths and skills

It is part of the SF approach to listen with a selective ear for skills and strengths a child or young person may mention. The coach can note these and remind the child or young person of them when they might prove useful.

Using strength cards can be another way to remind a child or young person of their resources. Strength cards can be looked through, chosen specifically or at random, and discussed. They offer a wide range of possibilities and a repertoire which might be familiar to the child but not yet articulated by them.

A further way to help children explore their skills and strengths is to suggest that they do some homework! This particular idea works well even with children who don't like homework. They are to be a reporter on a newspaper. The newspaper is about them, and they have to find as many people as possible to interview. They ask what each person appreciates about them in particular, and what skill or strength the person sees in them. They are encouraged to ask for stories, memories or anecdotes from the interviewee as examples. They write this up in a newspaper format. Putting things into words and saying things out loud makes a difference. Putting things on paper or into print also makes a difference.

young person to demonstrate qualities and skills which can be wonderful for them to hear themselves say out loud and useful for you to refer to during the session. Starting meetings on a positive, resourceful note can boost the overall effectiveness of any meeting. As Nancy Kline wrote, 'People think better throughout the meeting if the very first thing they do is to say something true and positive about their work or about how the work of the group is going' (Kline 1999: 107). This is also true of coaching sessions with children and young people. Starting coaching sessions with Resource Talk does seem, in my experience, to help children and young people to develop a mindset which is more open to possibilities, in themselves and others.

Best hopes: establishing a common aim

The person who wants the child to change in some way may not be the child himself/herself, it may be their teacher, parent or other professional or family member. Sometimes it is possible and appropriate to work with this concerned person alone, helping them to think about how they want to respond to, and manage, the child. At other times the coach may see the referring adult with the child, and talk about what they both want from the coaching for the child. At other times the coach may be working with a child alone.

Asking a child what their best hopes are from coaching does not always make sense to them; however, it is important to have a commission from the child for their coaching, even though this may be the child agreeing to someone else's ideas and wishes for them. If there is no genuine agreement about the focus for the work, the conversation can easily veer off track, with the coach finding themselves pushing the child towards whatever they believe to be best for them. So it is important to persevere at this stage. Rewording the question can be useful, for example: 'What would you notice that was different if coming here was useful to you?', 'How would you know if talking today turned out to be useful to you?' or 'What do you want to get better at?'. When it is still tricky for the child to identify

---

Best hopes scaling question

'How are things going for you at home/school/elsewhere? 10 means it's going OK/as well as you want, 1 is the opposite'.

- If a child says '10', then things seem to be fine, although you might want to ask what the child wants to notice about themselves which will keep them at 10.

- If a child says a lower number, your next question is: 'Would you like things to be going a bit better?'.

what they want from coaching, the coach can use a scaling question, because it can be easier for a child to answer, inviting the child to think about the different areas of their life and what is working well and not working so well.

Children (and adults) often frame their best hopes in a negative way, describing what they want to *stop* doing, and the coach can then ask the child what they would be doing *instead*. If the child mentions that they want another person to stop doing something it is important to check whether this should be explored and dealt with because it may be that someone is bullying or mistreating the child. If this is not the case, the coach can ask what difference it would make to the child if, for example, the teacher gave them more credits, or their friend didn't argue with them, to invite a different description of what they want to happen.

If what the child wants from coaching does not fit with the referring adult's concerns it is important for the child's best hopes to be acknowledged and honoured in the conversation if the child is to feel engaged in the process. Sometimes a child will repeat others' ideas without any ownership. For example, children might say 'pay more attention in class' or 'get better grades' or 'calm down' but without much interest. In these situations the coach can ask 'so in what way would that be good for you?' so that the child can explore what it actually means to them. The coach can also use a commitment scale so that the child can think about and say out loud how important or significant it is to them. What may of course matter to them is the approval of an adult or group. This is a legitimate contract of work with a child, though it is important to find out the details of the behaviour which would elicit the approval and what difference it would make to the child.

A commitment scale

If 10 means that you would do anything you can, whatever it takes, to realise and achieve this best hope, and 1 means that you don't care at all – you just said it for something to say – then where are you on this scale?

- How come you are there and not lower?

- What do you know about yourself which tells you that you can be there?

An agreed contract for coaching, whether with a child, young person or adult, has to be workable, that is, something that coaching can help with. This does not mean discouraging or crushing dreams, although it may mean a careful selection of elements of the child's dream. Being a famous film star or footballer can be explored; for example, what would the child like to be doing which would be small steps towards becoming a famous footballer? Alternatively, the question 'what difference would that make?' can sometimes lead to a redescription of the child's original ideas about what they wanted from coaching: 'I would be happier every day' or 'I would enjoy life more'.

What children want to change in their lives can at times appear insignificant in the context of all the difficulties which they are facing. However, working with children repeatedly proves that change in one area is often associated with change in another. As children begin to notice small changes that they are making, and believe that change is possible, they then seem able to tackle some of the other issues which they may be facing.

What children want from coaching needs to be safe and not harmful to themselves or others. It is important with children not to condone harmful wishes or behaviour so the coach may need to encourage the child to think about what they want in a different way. If necessary the coach will move out of an SF role, if safety or harmful behaviour is an issue, to do a safety assessment and agency referral; sometimes it can be appropriate to invite children to participate in talking about ideas of what will keep them safe, so that they learn the skills to recognise danger and to protect themselves.

Any 'best hopes' which a child expresses also need to incorporate possibility within them. For example, sometimes children say their best hope is 'never coming to school'. Some coaches may choose to invite more description of this by asking what difference it will make to the child; for example, the child might answer 'I'd be happier and less bored'. Then the coach will suggest: 'So you would like to be happier and more interested in things?' and this would become the contract. Other coaches might ask the child if never coming to school is a possibility; most children seem to understand that some form of schooling is compulsory. Then the coach might say: 'So if you have to come to school would you like to be happier when you are here?' and most children at this point would say they agree with this idea.

Example of staying with a child's 'best hopes'

I once worked with a child who I knew, from other professionals, found it very hard to keep calm and in control of his behaviour. The child told me he did not care about being calm and in control; what was most important to him was getting better at cleaning his football boots after every football match. This would help him play football better because the boots would look better, so he would feel more confident, and there would be no layers of caked dried mud on the boots, which made them very stiff to play in. So being able to play football better was what he wanted from coaching. In the session it turned out that playing football better involved many things, including him keeping his temper during and after matches.

Preferred futures

In asking children the details about their preferred future you are inviting them to describe what is meaningful to them in concrete detail. The preferred future becomes a landscape which sparkles for them, built of things which are significant and idiosyncratic to the child, connected to their own values, feelings and desires and not just tasks to be achieved. A child is much more likely to be motivated by this landscape, and the SF coach can remain at the child's side and avoid slipping into the tricky territory of task-orientated conversations.

In exploring preferred futures with children I have found that some children seem to like and respond to the Miracle Question whereas others seem to be happy with the more economical Tomorrow Question. Silence from the child can be a time to wait, to restate or to reformulate the question. Coaches like to develop their own styles in asking this question, or use different styles at different times, and it can be useful to ask this question slowly with pauses (de Shazer et al 2007: 42) when working with childen. This gives the question a story-like structure which is appealing to some children, giving them time to assimilate the idea and then carry on the story themselves. It is useful to be aware of what the word 'miracle' may mean to some children however. One child told me in the second session: 'The miracle happened, the miracle happened! I woke up, got out of bed, and didn't punch my brother even though he really annoyed me . . . I got dressed instead and ignored him . . . it won't happen again though . . . miracles only happen once!'.

A miracle question

I am going to ask you a strange question, this question needs us to put our imagination hats on . . . (we pretend to put hats on) . . . are you ready? . . . Suppose . . . when you go home tonight you do your usual things . . . have tea? . . . play? . . . go to a class? . . . do your homework? . . . watch TV? . . . (child nods or shakes head so that you get this bit right), then . . . you go to bed . . . and go to sleep . . . (pause here, this is the transition from the everyday to something more imaginary). While you are asleep . . . a miracle happens . . . and your best hopes start to happen in your life (or describe the child's best hopes, e.g. 'you are able to make friends/be calm/keep on with the concentration' etc.) . . . but you don't know this miracle has happened because you are asleep! When you wake up . . . what will be the first tiny signs that this miracle has happened . . . what will you first notice when you open your eyes, when you start to get ready for school . . . when you arrive at school . . .

For some children the Tomorrow Question will be enough to invite them into a conversation where they begin to describe, and in some ways inhabit, this future world during the session. Children will differ in how much detail they can provide of this world, but it is usually more than the coach might initially assume.

Some children might enjoy or might prefer to draw or write lists about what this future they desire will look like, and children who don't want to talk might like a friend or parent or teacher to speak for them, and describe what they think the child's best hopes will look like in practice. In my experience this often produces amusement and some correction from the child! Children can be asked what other people will notice when they have achieved what they wanted, and these 'other-person perspective' questions are often easy for children to answer, and can include real as well as fictional people, and animals too. Children are often very happy to enter into a more imaginative world, where 'relevant' famous or loved fictional characters might be noticing what will be different about the child's behaviour on the 'miracle' or 'tomorrow' day.

Scales

Scaling questions help the coach to enable the child to talk about their strengths and skills, what they want, what this will look like, and signs of progress, trusting the child to know what they are talking about, without it necessarily being clear to the coach. Many coaches use a numerical scale of 0 to 10; however, with children, I have always preferred to use a numerical scale of 1 to 10, which is the range of numbers even quite young children are able to count. Scales can operate as an agreed code, but the child is the code breaker so they remain in charge. The coach sets the bench marks, the child sets the values and the progress, and – in a world where they are often marked by others – children often enjoy this. Children seem to understand scales easily, and whereas adults sometimes think or rethink where they are on a scale, children will often answer speedily in numbers and fractions of numbers. One child I worked with always worked in numbers and 20ths of numbers ('I am at 5 and 4/20').

However, scales with children don't have to be constructed with number values, they can be made of different foods, faces, ladders, snakes etc. I enjoy constructing scales with children which challenge the idea that change is going to be hard work, an uphill, mountain-climbing activity. I have used ski slopes, down the side of mountains, ever-increasing snowballs, fast-flowing rivers, slides and swings. The top end of the scale can be the child's 'best hopes' described, if possible, as a cluster of possibilities, so that it can include a rich palette of changes and not the dullness of specific tasks. The other end of the scale can be kept vague if possible (I often say 'the opposite') – why waste time describing something you don't want to see? Subscales and multiple scales can also be used, breaking down what the child wants to see into different components or dealing with a multiplicity of issues without the need for the child to prioritise them. However the scale is constructed, it is a concrete sign to the child that they are going somewhere – they can point, walk or jump to the next point (depending on how you set up the scale).

Children often answer the question 'how come you are at 4 (say) and not lower?' with a description of why they are there and not higher, i.e. a list of what they are *not* doing. It is useful to be on the alert for this, and to interrupt it if necessary by repeating the question. On the other hand, it is possible to dwell happily on the question for much longer than may at first seem possible. This is a time to ask what else, what else, what else ... If the child is going to notice something they haven't noticed before, it might take some time and energy to see it. I like to spend just a little time on the next signs, perhaps asking about one or two. If the coach is too eager and keen to collect a whole heap of signs, the child may start to feel a little pushed or pulled up the scale. The process seems more to me that change begins to emerge for the child – they start to see it happening and this gives them the buoyancy to see more and do more. When scaling questions are used with children, the landscape becomes one of footprints as well as pathways, showing the parts of the wished-for future that the child is already doing, with more and more opportunities opening up on the horizon.

Examples of scales

- **Preferred-future scales**. 10 is ... (whatever the child has described, the details of their best hopes from the work), and 1 is the opposite
- **Confidence scales** (of achieving their best hopes)
- **Commitment scales**. 10 means that you really really really want to do this; 1 means that you are just saying it but you don't much care ... (children seem to love this scale, and it is useful for them to think about whether their commitment is high or low).
- **Coping scales** (when children are finding change difficult and are just getting through)
- **Effort scales**. 10 means that you are going to put as much effort as you can into this, and 1 means that you are going to put into this as little effort as you have ever put into anything. (Again, it is useful for children to hear themselves answer this.)
- **Other-person perspective scales**. Asking the child where their friend, parent, teacher etc. would put them on any of the above scales. Sometimes children seem to find it easier to think about themselves from others' points of view.

Molehills and mountains: the magic of words

Steve de Shazer wrote about the magical power of words and how language works in therapy (de Shazer 1994). SF coaches know that the words they use make a difference: they can close or open opportunities, increase or decrease optimism, maximise or minimise resources, and create a climate for stuckness or change. In this, as in many things, the maxim 'be careful what you ask for, you just might get it' is useful to keep in mind. For example, using the word 'step' makes things seem harder work, and needing completion, whereas using the word 'sign' is lighter, more open and suggests that the beginnings are enough to talk about in a session. In a similar way, saying 'what will you *have to* notice' suggests things are going to be tough, whereas saying 'what *will* you notice' assumes that change will happen.

A change of tense can make sweeping generalisations into one-off behaviours. For example, if a child says 'I can't play football' this is closed and final, but if you repeat back to the child 'You haven't been able to play football in the past' the change of tense operates as a ray of hope. Conversely, you can change such statements into sweeping generalisations when they are good for the child. For example, if a child says to you 'I played a good match today' then you can ask 'What did this tell you about yourself?' with the possible answer 'I am the sort of person who can play good matches'. This is an 'identity question' which begins to add depth to one-off behaviours and so makes them seem more possible and repeatable to the child.

Future dreams can be located in past achievements:

'I want to be able to make friends in secondary school.'

'Tell me about a time when you made friends before.'

And past failures can be a springboard for the future:

'I used to be a bully in year 4.'

'So what made you decide to do something different?'

Gaps and pauses

Most children understand the rules about fairness and turn taking, particularly as they relate to the rhythm of conversations. Just as they will feel unheard if your next question does not relate to their previous answer, so they will understand that it is their turn to speak when you stop speaking. It is useful to keep this in mind during a coaching session.

If a child does not answer a question immediately I often construe this in my mind as their thinking time, and I model this by sometimes leaving a gap for thinking myself about the next question I am going to ask. I might comment that it's good to think about questions and answers, and then wait with an expectant look and smile on my face. In many situations the child will understand the wait as their turn to speak. Thinking time allows them to come up with answers which they had to search for, answers they might not have thought about before, and which are therefore potentially more useful to them. If the coach thinks that the child is feeling uncomfortable with the gap, then they can rephrase the question a few times. If the child says 'I don't know' the coach can ask 'and if you did know?' or 'have a guess' or 'what might you think?' or ask about someone who knows them well and enquire what that person might say. Children are often happier than we might think to sit in a pause, and a pause can often show that the questions are working because the child is thinking. If the child is really uncomfortable in a pause the coach can choose to deal with this appropriately by asking a different question. However, a further silence can still prove useful to the child. SF questions are there for the child and not the coach; we do not need to 'find out' anything, and often the questions can do their job just as well, even if the child does not answer, because he or she will be thinking about them.

Pace

Children often enjoy attention, especially one-to-one if they can experience being heard, finding their competencies, skills and confidence, and expressing their wishes and hopes. So talking about what they can do and what they want to do is likely to be attractive to them. I have watched as children seem to blossom and take up more space before me as they talk.

However, children are also actively bored when things do not interest them: averting their eyes, fidgeting, and doing something else. This in itself will disconnect them from the ongoing conversation even if it were shortly to be potentially more interesting to them. Therefore it is important when coaching children to be aware of the pace of the session, when to listen, linger, explore and wait for answers, and when to conduct things at a more cracking pace. The younger the child the shorter your session is likely to be, the older the child the longer the session can be, until you get to teenagers, when you may find a return to shorter sessions works best. And many sessions take place in environments where time is limited. However, the impact of the coaching is not so necessarily limited. The child does some work in the session, but a lot more outside of it.

Lists

Asking for more than one example of progress is a way of adding breadth to the changes already made. Questions seeking breadth and depth locate the changes more firmly in the child's repertoire, so that they are less likely to seem like one-off examples which happened by luck. One effective way to do this is to introduce lists into your questions. Children respond very well to making lists of things. For example, in the second and subsequent sessions you will be interested in what the child has noticed is going better for them in the sphere of their best hopes. 'Tell me something you have been pleased to notice you have been doing recently' can sometimes work less well than: 'Tell me 10 things – no, *20* things – you have been pleased to notice . . . ', especially if you produce paper and pens/crayons to record this or even ready-made blank lists (Chapter 8). Perhaps the longer list means that more arbitrary or less apparently serious items can be added; certainly it can help children to think of more answers, and it is often those answers which don't come to the fore of their minds immediately which can be most useful to them. So it is the 20th thing which might be most useful since it was most hidden. And it can be fun for children to do.

Very long lists can be produced, adding breadth and depth to descriptions of strengths/qualities/progress by utilising the following different types of question:

- What have you (the child) noticed?
- What have others noticed? (multi-perspectival)
- Where have you noticed these changes? (multiple contexts)
- Russian dolls: unpack one answer to discover many more: e.g. 'I am a good friend', 'Tell me five things you do which make you a good friend'.

Endings

The length of a session with a child might be predetermined by the context you are working in as well as the age and needs of the child. Depending on time factors, as well as on the session itself, you may want to include some of the following in how you end your session with a child:

1   Acknowledging the difficulties the child has experienced.
2   Giving compliments which are accurate and connected to the child's best hopes. Children are often perceptive and sensitive about their strengths and weaknesses; an ill-judged compliment will slide away from their attention, an honest compliment will root and grow.
3   Giving compliments which fit with your role, for example, not complimenting anything which in your professional role you would not be able to approve of.
4   Highlighting any qualities the child has mentioned which fit with the likelihood of their achieving their best hopes.
5   Highlighting what the child is already doing that is useful.
6   Offering 'noticing suggestions', for example: 'I want you to notice anything which is telling you that you are moving up your scale/moving in the right direction/becoming even more confident (or whatever the child is wanting from the sessions)'. It is sometimes helpful to focus children's attention in this way before they leave the session, but to keep the objects of the focus quite broad so that the possibilities are kept wide open.

On occasion I ask children if there is a particular thought or idea that they will be taking away with them from the meeting.

There are certain factors which mean that ending a piece of work *overall* does not usually take on the significance that it holds in other approaches, and therefore there may be a variety of ways the piece of work comes to an end and not a 'right' way to construct the ending.

In SFBC the relationship between child and coach is important but the focus is never on this relationship, but on the child's own everyday life. The coach is interested in the child noticing change, who else notices change in the child's life, how the child will respond to that person, and what difference that will make. The child's own life sparkles, the coach operates in the shade. In addition, the agent for change is the child. The child decides on the change they want to make, what it will look like, what signs they might notice and then when they have made progress. In this way the coach is not a central part of change in the child's mind. Children often say to me 'I did it myself'. It is this invisibility of the coach which is an essential part of the approach. Insoo Kim Berg summed this up by advising practitioners (in personal communications and in conferences) to leave no footprints in the client's life.

Endings therefore operate in a different way in SFBC. Children sometimes finish coaching by not coming to the next session. An SF coach will see this as the child knowing best when they have had enough, and believes that the child will go on doing the work themselves outside and beyond the sessions. The focus does not need to be on a child having a 'final session' but on a child getting on with their own everyday life.

However, even with the emphasis on the centrality of the child's own life rather than on the sessions, some children do find endings difficult when they are ready to stop coaching. One child said to me: 'When you ask me these questions I hear myself answer and then I know what I'm going to do so who's going to ask me the questions now?' She was right in that she had all the answers, and so we talked about how she could ask herself the questions.

As with other approaches, children learn the 'rules' of any approach quickly. Often children will come to subsequent sessions armed with answers to the 'what's been better' question, or answer a scaling question before it's even asked. Learning to be SF in their approach to challenges can be a useful life skill for children to take away with them when sessions end.

Using materials (Chapter 8) – such as credit cards, stickers, posters, lists and mind maps – is a concrete reminder to children of their own resources, and it can help those who might find final sessions tricky. Many children have told me how they have their cards or posters on their bedroom wall as a concrete reminder of their strengths and skills and what they have achieved.

Endings are beginnings too. I sometimes think with children about the most important things they want to keep doing, knowing that this will lead to new things as well. In addition to seeing the end of something as having the seeds of new things, SFBC of course starts the first session with the end in mind. The whole approach has a cyclical movement: familiar things can be rediscovered with new aspects, and new things can be familiar too. This idea is particularly useful in working with children, meeting their twin needs for security and risk taking.

Case examples

Brenda, 10

Brenda came with her mother, Judith, who was worried that her daughter seemed unhappy some of the time, and was not achieving what she was capable of in school.

We started with 'resource talk', with Brenda telling me a bit about herself, what she liked doing, her favourite TV programmes and games she liked to play. I gave Brenda some cards, which included activities, skills and qualities, and invited her to look through them and begin to choose some about herself.

Brenda chose lots of cards which she spread about her on the floor – cards showing things she was good at, things she liked doing, things she might do more of, and Judith joined in, adding more to the piles. Both were surprised, and enjoyed the activity. It provided a springboard for finding out Brenda's many skills and strengths, served as a 'warm up' activity, and set the tone for the sort of conversation we might be having – one of resources rather than deficits. Judith said that Brenda had agreed to come to the session because she did not feel very happy at school. She said she would like her to be happier. When asked more about what she hoped would be different in her life as a result of the coaching, Brenda said that she would also like to feel more confident about herself in school. We spent a lot of the session exploring how Brenda would know that she was happier and more confident in school. Some of her ideas included:

- *I would get along with more people, and maybe I would speak to people more.*
- *I would answer some questions in class.*
- *I would tell mum more about my school day on the way home.*
- *I would work a bit harder in school.*
- *I'd sometimes get my head down sooner.*
- *I'd move my hand faster across the page when I am writing.*
- *I would focus more of the time, then I would get better grades.*
- *I might feel OK about trying things I can't do yet, like swimming, and not be so scared.*
- *I would try harder in football, maybe even tackle sometimes.*

We did some scales, first an overall scale for confidence and happiness at school made of different foods Brenda liked in order of preference (10 was pizza, 9 chocolate ice cream, 8 pasta and so on). We also did some subscales: Brenda chose a ladder for talking more to people in school and to her mum; and a thermometer, for working harder, getting her head down and writing faster etc. Overall, Brenda was at 4 for confidence and happiness at school, and was higher for the subscales. Brenda, assisted by Judith, found lots of good reasons why she was at those numbers and not lower, a list which surprised them both. I then asked Brenda for one sign that would tell her she was moving up her scale and she said: 'I might say 'hi' to Renee first thing when I arrive in school, and smile' (Renee was a popular girl she wanted to be friends with).

In the second and subsequent sessions we concentrated on what Brenda had been pleased to notice about her confidence and happiness. We took to making long lists, 10 or 20 things, small things and big things, things she had noticed and others had noticed. Children often like to talk about what others have noticed; adults often give them feedback, and it is easy for them to report compliments. Mr Whales, a teacher, had noticed that she was concentrating a bit more in her maths and literacy lessons, mum had noticed that she was trying to finish her homework, Renee had responded to her morning greetings with an invitation to play at break, and the football coach had noticed her efforts to tackle in football practice.

After the third session, Brenda reported that she was all right now, she 'knew how to do it', things were a lot better for her, and she didn't want to come any more. Judith was in agreement, although she would have preferred to book another session in the future. However, children are very present-orientated, and Brenda had better things to do: working harder, playing sports and making friends. She had already learned that many of the skills involved in her wishes for the future were familiar to her, and that others were possible to develop.

Anna, 9

Anna came to coaching sessions as part of a programme offered to her class in school. In her first session her best hope was to focus more on her work: she would be looking at her teacher more in class, writing more pages of work, and doing her homework in less time at home. Her best friend would notice some of these things first and would be telling her 'well done' and this would make her feel proud and make her feel like she was the kind of person who could get certificates. She would also have more time to play at home.

By the second session she had noticed that she was producing a bit more work, and her teacher had commented on this. She was also doing her homework faster and sometimes answering a question in class, because she was concentrating more on what the teacher was saying. This had made her feel more confident about herself and she noticed that she was also talking to other children a bit more, children who were not her friends. Anna thought she would like to express herself even more. She was noticing new changes she had not originally described; and if she had been tied down to goals and action plans these changes might have been squeezed out of her attention. Instead, the breadth of possibilities for change became wider. So, in session 3 we explored what expressing herself more meant for her; it included answering questions in a louder voice, giving her views in class discussions, and getting on with activity partners in class. She role-played with me how she and her activity partner would behave, and how she would look at her partner (rather than look away all the time) and try to be helpful; I role-played how her partner might respond. Then we changed roles and discovered even more details. I asked her to role-play what her teacher might notice too, and she showed her teacher saying how well Anna and her partner were working together and how they were smiling more. In later sessions we talked about what this had told her about herself – 'I'm getting a bit more confident' – and how she had done this: 'I told myself not to worry about what people think'. Scales were useful in encouraging even more detail: signs of progress included being heard on the other side of the room, and making eye contact with people.

Anna always took her time to answer questions in the coaching sessions. However, every answer was sparkling, and her sessions always reminded me to wait respectfully while she had time to think. It was also interesting that she always put herself quite high on the scales, usually 7 or 8, and this led me to assume that there were probably even more exceptions or instances of success that I had not heard, and reminded me that the value of each number on the scale is personal to the child. The scale provides a means of talking about change. I have noticed that other children sometimes put themselves in perhaps surprising places on a scale; I have learnt to enjoy the surprise.

Comments from children on coaching

Coaching is really good for me, the sessions encourage me, and I can't speak like this anywhere else. It helps me to talk in coaching, I don't realise what I think until I put it into words then things seem better.

When I tell you what I'm doing then I do it more.

I like the sessions because I can talk about things. Usually I have to keep things stuffed inside me but here I can talk about things, bad and good things.

It gave me a boost to get the life I imagined and be more confident in class.

References

Berg, I.K. and Steiner, T. (2003) *Children's Solution Work*. New York: W.W. Norton.

de Shazer, S. (1994) *Words Were Originally Magic*. New York: W.W. Norton.

de Shazer, Steve, Dolan, Yvonne, Korman, Harry, Trepper, Terry, MacCollum, Eric and Berg, Insoo Kim (2007) *More Than Miracles: The State of the Art of Solution Focused Therapy*. New York: Haworth.

Kline, N. (1999) *Time To Think*. London: Ward Lock.

Selekman, Matthew, D (1997) *Solution-Focused Therapy With Children*. New York: Guildford Press.
Szabo, P. (2006) Solution Focused Use of Scaling Questions (Strengthening Your Coaching Competency To Ask Powerful Questions). Presentation for UK ICF, November, Regent's College London.

Adolescents

Adolescents are regarded as a particularly challenging group to work with. They seem to be in a constant state of trying to 'find themselves', dealing with peer-group pressures, with emergent sexuality and sexual identity, defying authority . . . and they have a dire propensity to say 'don't know' to whatever they're asked.

Ah, that 'don't know'. There are times when one is talking with an adolescent and it seems as if 'don't know' is said as a sort of instinctive response – at least when an adult is on the receiving end. We have known young people who say 'don't know' automatically and then pause to think of a response. It's like a safe option, as in 'I'll say "don't know" and then consider whether in fact I want to answer the question'. Given the nature of so many of the questions they are asked, maybe that's just a wise strategy! For example:

Parent: Where have you been?
Young person: Out
P: Where is out?
YP: A place
P: So, who were you with?
YP: People (Berg & Steiner 2003: 196)

Karen, 14

Karen came for an initial session in a school. This is how the conversation started:

Coach: What are your best hopes from this meeting?
Karen: Don't know.
Coach: What will tell you it's been useful?
Karen: Don't know.
Coach: What are you hoping it will lead to?
Karen: Don't know.
Coach (*getting more desperate*): How will you know it's not been a waste of time?
Karen: Don't know.

So far, so predictable. I was following our procedure, to try to prioritise the young person's hopes and wishes. And getting nowhere. Some people would even suggest that asking young people what they want is pointless. This is because the vast majority of young people are involuntary clients, in the sense that their attendance is being done as a favour to someone else or has been forced upon them – and so, even when they are asked what they want, they assume (often quite rightly) that it's only a matter of time before the adult *tells* them what is wanted.

In that case, the next step suggests itself. If the young person has been *sent* then one can ask them why they've been sent ... but this isn't likely to be productive because that is asking them to admit to problems and so it is likely that you will just get more 'don't knows'. The better question is to ask what a *significant other* is hoping will come out of the meeting. In the example above, I paused to think about which 'significant other' to introduce. Who, I wondered, is the most important person in the life of the average 14-year-old?

Coach: How will your friends know it's not been a waste of time?
Karen: I won't be so unhappy.

The door has now been opened. As Karen has answered in terms of a negative, it makes sense to look for an alternative:

Coach: How would they know that?
Karen: I would talk to them.

This gives the coach much to work with. There are many possible questions at this point, such as 'Where would you talk? What would you talk about? Who might you talk to first? Which of your friends would be most pleased about you talking to them? How would you know they liked it? What effect would that have on you?'. These are questions which have the effect of 'zooming in' on the scenario to elicit more detail. A different approach is to 'zoom out', to go for a panoramic view:

Coach: You would talk to them. What else?
Karen: I'd focus on my work more.

This answer might seem surprising until one remembers the context: the meeting was taking place in a school.

The perspective of significant others

It is impossible to underestimate the power of third-party questions with young people. Another 'significant other' is, obviously, the referrer, and the coach in the above example could have decided to ask 'How will your teacher/tutor/

mentor/parent know that it's not been a waste of time?'. The question arises as to what to do if the client keeps on saying 'don't know' to whoever is being introduced into the conversation. In our experience it is very rare not to finally get an answer from *someone's* perspective about what is wanted, but if that happens there may be no option but to suggest to the young person that the meeting is postponed until it is possible to gauge the opinion of a third party. A three-way meeting including the referrer (or person most concerned) may be necessary. In one case a teacher accompanied a 12-year-old to the session. When I asked the young man what his best hopes were, I got the 'don't know' answer, which surprised me, as it is usual that – when there is a referring adult present – the young person will 'own up' as to what's wanted. I then asked 'What do you think are Mr Smith's best hopes from this meeting?' and was even more surprised when he said 'don't know'. Perhaps the young man assumed that the adults would sooner or later start discussing him over his head, so he was just waiting for me to turn to the teacher, which I had no option but to do. Obviously, the reason for giving the young person the opportunity to answer first is that it gives them the chance to answer for themselves; it shows that we are genuinely interested in their views, so that if they choose not to answer, we have in any case made it clear that this is important to us. If, however, we have to start from the referrer's wishes, then, although that is better than nothing, we are still in the position of having to find a way to get back to the young person's wishes. We might ask them to say what the teacher (for example) is hoping to see them doing, and then clarify 'Would that be good for *you*?' followed by '*How* would that be good for you?'. Even if they were to say only 'they'd get off my back' that is, at least, a start. 'How would it be good for you if they were off your back? What difference would that make to you?' And suddenly we have the beginnings of a motivated young person wanting things to be different!

Ahmed, 14

A 14-year-old student called Ahmed is brought to the interview room by a teacher who had found him wandering in the corridors (rather than coming on time for his appointment). I ask about his best hopes from the meeting, and there follows a bout of 'don't knows' and 'not sures'. I then ask what the referrer, who was his learning mentor, would want to see and Ahmed says 'I wouldn't be running in the corridors'.

Coach: So if you weren't running, what would you be doing?
Ahmed: Probably talking to friends, and walking.
Coach: So you'd be talking to friends, you'd be walking. What else would he see?
Ahmed: Not shouting.
Coach: So you'd be talking to friends instead of shouting?

Ahmed: Yes, because I normally shout across the hall.
Coach: Do you? OK. So what would you do instead of shouting across the hall?
Ahmed: Walk to the person.
Coach: Oh I see. If you saw someone you wanted to talk to, instead of shouting across you'd walk across.

I keep reflecting back what I'm hearing to ensure I'm getting it exactly right. I then check out whether Ahmed's friends would be 'amazed' at this change in behaviour and he says 'they might do'.

Coach: Would they be pleased?
Ahmed: Probably, because they say I give them earache.

This represents a turning point from my perspective. Up to this point, it isn't clear whether the differences in behaviour Ahmed is referring to are ones that he knows people want of him – how many times has he been told 'don't shout!' 'don't run!' – or ones that he actually wants for himself. The news that even his friends are telling him to quieten down points to a change that Ahmed himself might genuinely want, namely, to keep his friends happy.

Coach: So it would be good for them not to get earache. How would it be good for *you*, if you weren't giving people earache, you weren't shouting in the corridors . . .
Ahmed: I won't get into trouble.

This is the classic response from young people who others have concerns about. What is in it for a young person to change their behaviour? Most times they think that what they do is either fine in itself or shouldn't bother others. So their motivation is not towards changing what they do. But if the outcome of change is that they will have less hassle in their lives, then this might be motivation enough. In Ahmed's case, it turns out that his behaviour has led to him being monitored on report cards, which involve teachers rating his performance in every lesson, and the card has to be signed by his mother each day. It was interesting that Ahmed had not referred to any problems in lessons.

Coach: It sounds like you want to get off those report cards. Why's that?
Ahmed: It's annoying!
Coach: Would your parents be pleased if you weren't on report?
Ahmed: Yeah.
Coach: What would they say?
Ahmed: Not sure.
Coach: How would you know they were pleased?
Ahmed: They'd get me stuff . . . let me take out money and buy sweets and things I like.

This whole session lasted all of 12 minutes and this was adequate time to enable Ahmed to clarify that there really would be benefits to him in changing his behaviour without me having to make any suggestions whatsoever, and by session 2 (which, again, he failed to show up to and had to be brought to) he was already on the way to coming off the report cards.

At your best

Despite what it says in the textbooks, including this one, the course of SFBC sessions does not usually run smoothly as the following case will demonstrate.

Janice, 16

Janice was a 16-year-old 'looked after child'. She was accompanied to BRIEF by Maria, the manager of the unit where she was resident, and Cathy, a specialist child-care worker, arriving an hour late because she hadn't been at the meeting point arranged with Maria. I asked her if she had any questions before we started and she said 'How can you talking to me help me do anything? My mum can talk to me, my family, Maria can talk to me. I don't see the point of it'. I explained that this coaching method has been found to be useful and that I would try my best to make it so 'but there are no guarantees'. I then asked her what her best hopes were from coming to see me, and she shrugged and said 'don't know'. I tried rephrasing the question but got nowhere. Bearing in mind that she had said she could talk with her mother, I asked her what would tell her mother that coming to see me had been useful but still made no progress, as she said her mother felt she was 'fine'. I tried to press on with asking about her mother's hopes but Janice started to look irritated and stopped answering. As Cathy had set up the meeting, I changed to asking Janice what Cathy's best hopes were, and after a couple of 'don't knows' she said 'Go to college. Probation, I think. Can't remember the rest'. This seemed like a move in the right direction of establishing a 'contract' for our work. I asked her what she wanted to study at college and she said 'childcare'. I tried to establish whether we also needed to talk about probation. She wasn't sure. Cathy interjected that 'these are all things she is supposed to do' and we went back to talking about college.

Coach: So you *want* to go to college?
Janice: It's one of the things I want to do, but I can't be arsed to.
Coach: You want to go to college but you can't be arsed to. So help me here. You want to go to college?
Janice: When I wake up in the morning I think of better things to do.

She proceeded to complain about the things she was being asked to do, like 'go on probation', and how 'I'm fed up having to compromise all the time'.

Coach: So, do you want it to be different in future? Do you want to wake up in the morning and do what *you* want to do?

Janice: Obviously I'd want to do it but I can't be bothered, I'm just tired.

Coach: So at the moment you're tired and what you really want to do is get up in the morning and do what you want to do.

Janice: Yeah, obviously.

Coach: How long have you been doing what you don't want to do . . .

Janice (*interrupting*): All my life.

Coach: No, feeling tired and not wanting to get up; how long has that been going on?

Janice: About 4 years.

Coach: About 4 years. So what you want to do, is be able to go to college, and *want* to do it, and not feel tired, and that's going to be a big change in your life.

Janice: Yeah.

Coach: Wow!

I then turned to Cathy:

Cathy: My hopes from today are to help Janice to do what she wants to do. She's so creative: every time we meet she's making things; every time we start off with just a little something and by the end of the hour there's so much there, and Janice has said that she wants to go to college to do creative things. So my best hopes from today are that there could be a little movement, a little encouragement for Janice to move towards . . .

Janice (*interrupting*): People are on my case everyday. I just want time to be quiet, time to think.

I merely said 'okay' to this and turned to Maria and asked her about her hopes from this.

Maria: My hope is for her to be happy with what's she's doing, and it would last, because she'd feel happy and excited about something. In the morning it's like she said, so it's getting the motivation going but once it's going it'd be OK. It's like coming here. She doesn't want to come but once she comes and gets involved with things, it's OK.

Coach: Right.

Maria: So it's hoping it will be something she'll just get up and do rather than that slow kind of train . . .

Janice (*interrupting*): I feel like people are treating me like I'm not normal. That's the person I am, I'm just lazy, innit.

Maria: I don't think you're lazy.

Janice: Not lazy, but I've never been bothered to do anything in the mornings.

Coach: You're not a morning person?

Janice: No, I'd sleep until 4 o'clock if I could.

Coach: But is that something you want for yourself, or . . .

Janice: I don't see why not!

Coach: Yes, and you say that you want to do what you want to do and be free to do what you want to do. I guess I'm curious about the college thing.

Janice: If there's college, and there's financial help, I have to go there, then obviously I'll go. That's what I said last year, and I was OK for the first two months, and then they kicked me out from the course because of my punctuality.

Coach: So you went for a couple of months! And you're up for trying this again?

Janice: Yeah, I have to or else I'll be dumb.

Coach: And you don't want to be dumb.

Janice: Obviously!

Coach: So, from what I'm hearing, you're a very creative person, someone with talents, you get things done, and it's getting going that's important to you, and if you get going you can get stuff done, and you want to give college another go. And that's important to you because you don't want to be dumb.

I was beginning to feel we were making progress. We'd found what she was motivated towards, and now I thought we could firm up the contract by focusing on college itself. I thought we could explore her preferred future in terms of things going well for her on her course – well enough that she would want to continue through the whole year. I decided to focus on the first day of term, mindful that, as the session was taking place in August, college could feel very far off for her.

Coach: When's the first day of college?

Janice: I may not get in the college. I have to do an assessment. I have to do that first before I can go.

Maria: It's on Saturday.

Janice: I might not be able to go to college.

This threw me. Suddenly there was doubt about her even getting a place on the course.

Coach: Oh, you've got to do an assessment in order to get into college, and that's this Saturday. And you're up to doing it?

Janice: I don't *want* to do it but I have to because I don't want to be thick.

At this point I had to make a choice. I could have ignored the assessment meeting and continued to talk about things going well on the course, in the hope that that would then strengthen her desire to do whatever it took to get there. But I decided instead that we could focus on her getting through the assessment, as it was obviously more immediate and I wasn't sure that talking about things more distant – that might not happen – would engage her. I asked about the nature of the assessment, and she said felt sure she was 'dumber' than before. I asked her how confident she was of getting on the course and she said '45% – not 100%!' (this was said spontaneously; I hadn't asked her to give a figure). I asked her how come it was even that much and she said that 'maybe they will like me' even though her test results would be no better than a year ago. I asked if there was anything she might be able to do between the day of our meeting (Tuesday) and Saturday to prepare but she said there was no point: 'It would be a waste of time and I don't like wasting my time'. This spurred me on to ask about Saturday itself.

Coach: Let's say that when you wake up Saturday morning, it turns out to be a day when you're at your best; how will you know you're going to do the best job you can?

Janice: I don't need to know. Obviously I'll try my hardest. I don't need to know (*sitting back, yawning*).

Coach: Let's put it this way. How will Maria know on Saturday you're up for it and you're at your best?

Janice: Because I'll get ready.

Coach: OK. And what time will that be, Saturday morning?

Janice: I've got to be there at 10, so 9, I don't know, 8, 7 . . .

Coach: What time would you *like* her to see you?

Janice: 6.

It turned out that Maria was not going to be on duty that morning. I asked how the worker that morning would know Janice was at her best but Janice said the worker 'don't know me, she wouldn't know'. So I asked her how *she* would know she was at her best and she said that she would have had enough sleep, and 'I would be using my brain'. But she added 'you can never know you're at your best until you do it'. So I asked her to rate the day, with (using her percentage idea) '100% this is the most important day in your life right now and 0 the opposite' and she said '100%!'. I was suitably impressed and she explained that she'd like to go to university like her brother had. I asked her to rate her confidence that if she got a place she would 'pull it off' to get through the course, and she said 45%, which, of course, led to questions from me about how come that much.

We were out of time and I was unable to amplify descriptions as much as I would have liked; for example, as to how impressed her friends would be with her if she did her best on Saturday. As the above segments of the transcript show, the session tended to chop and change about. It was by no means a 'model' SF meeting in the style outlined in Chapter 1.

Maria and Cathy decided it had been such hard work getting Janice to the session at BRIEF that there were no further appointments. However, in the following April I received an email from Cathy: 'I wanted to let you know that Janice had found the session useful last year and her comments were as follows: "I don't know what that man done but I felt happier afterwards and I managed to go to college after that"'.

When things appear not to improve

Josh, 15, and Beth

Another case illustrates an important SF principle, that change can be started anywhere in a client's life, and therefore doesn't have to be specifically connected to the problem that is being dealt with. A 15-year-old, Josh, attended a meeting with his mother, Beth, because since the Easter holidays he had stopped going to school. At the start of the first meeting I asked him what his hopes were from coming and he said 'me go in a bit more often, and then consistently'. As it was Friday afternoon I asked the Tomorrow Question, starting with Monday morning to explore his preferred future on a school day in detail, and looked at the differences his getting to school would make to him, his family, friends and teachers. Then we looked at where he was on a progress scale. He said that when he walked through the door at BRIEF he'd have said 3. However, 'I've talked to other people and this has been much better' and said that now he was at '5 or 6'. We looked in detail at what told him that. I didn't ask him about moving up the scale, but given his comment about going into school 'a bit more often' I asked him how confident he was that he would manage to go in *one* day in the next week and he said '9'. We arranged to meet again a week later.

However, a few days later Beth called up to say that Josh hadn't gone to school and she was asking for their next appointment to be brought forward. When they arrived I told Josh that I understood that he hadn't returned to school 'yet'. I acknowledged Beth's disappointment and said that nevertheless I was interested in even the smallest differences they had noticed since we met. He said 'yes, there have been *some* differences', saying that he had been eating breakfast with the rest of the family and also had been talking more to his mother. I asked him what he thought of these things and he said 'I like it being different; change is good, it means it's not always bad'. His mother said that these were hopeful signs and that their relationship had improved, as there was less arguing and rudeness. We then revisited his scale, which was now at '4 or 5' but had been '8 or 9' at the weekend. His confidence of going back to school in the next week was still high (8) and so I asked some more questions about the differences it would make to his life if he were to be back at school ('I'd feel proud and happy, a sense of achievement, at ease . . . '). Then I asked Beth what she might notice about him at the weekend that would be signs that she could be hopeful about him going back to school. I also asked what his friends would notice. He was adamant that he wouldn't answer their questions about whether he was going back to school and that he preferred to keep doing things in order not to talk about it. I reflected that he had been under a lot of pressure and it seemed to me that he had considerable strength of will. He agreed, and we looked at ways he was using his strength. He listed 'pushing myself' to do things he liked such as sports and going out to see his friends more, and talked about wanting to do things around the house such as cleaning, washing and cooking chores.

At the end we made an arrangement to meet 2 weeks later. On the day of the next appointment Beth called asking to cancel because Josh had returned to school!

Beth had been, understandably, very concerned about her son's non-attendance – to the extent that, when she called the office to enquire about an initial appointment, she asked us whether we would do a home visit because she doubted she could get Josh to leave the house to come to BRIEF. Although I hadn't ignored the issue of school attendance, I had avoided asking any questions about the *process* of actually getting into school. In the second session, after acknowledging that he felt under growing pressure from the school, friends and family to go back, I emphasised that only he would know when the right time was to do that and maybe it was good for him to continue to work on other achievements and interests he had that would be important to him in life no matter what. I approached the session with the belief that, as no one does their problems 24 hours a day, there will be some signs of success, however small; without that belief, I would, following Beth's pessimistic phone call, have come to the meeting fearing that maybe change wasn't possible for this young man (as there are no guarantees in this work!). In which case I might have had to renegotiate the contract for the work (such as a focus on how they might cope in future with him not attending school), or fired myself. As it is, the successful outcome to this case was unrelated to knowing anything about *why* he had stopped going to school (they said nothing about it and I never asked), nor to any focus on what 'needed to be done' to get him to school.

Challenging behaviours

Some young people have to endure extremely tough situations that they are powerless to do anything about, and a useful position to take is that there are good ways to cope with a bad situation and bad ways to do so. However, if a client says that what helps them to cope is something that others would regard as harmful, such as behaviours like cutting or excess alcohol or drug consumption, then this provides a challenge for the coach who wants to remain non-judgmental and client-centred. With the 'duty of care' we owe young people it is inappropriate to stay neutral in such situations, and it may be necessary to engage in some sort of 'risk assessment' – or refer to someone who can. If the young person has no idea that what they are doing is harmful then some coaches may take the view that they should try to educate them as to what the dangers are, and may, on the basis of the responses they get, decide that they need to report the matter elsewhere. But in the vast majority of cases the young person is fully aware of the risks they are taking and are hearing repeatedly to that effect from concerned adults. In such a situation, it is pointless for the coach to add their voice to what the young person is already hearing from others. Instead, it may be useful to say 'you must have a good reason to do X' (Berg & Steiner op. cit.: 133). If a client is asked 'How is it helpful to you to do X?' this respects their self-agency, indicating that you understand that they aren't stupid (whatever other people might be saying to or about them) and that you want to understand what they hope to achieve *from* the behaviour. Young people who self-harm often say that this activity helps them to cope with things better. As one client said, 'I cut myself so that I won't feel the pain', meaning mental pain. This leads to a conversation about how coping better looks and feels like to them before the coach can move on to discuss what the client knows about other ways of self-soothing (and can offer suggestions if that would be appropriate). There is no guarantee that this will lead the young person away from self-harming behaviour immediately (and slips are common with behaviours that have become habitual) but it is likely to be more effective than the educational or health-based approach that most probably has already been tried.

Taneesha, 16

A 16-year-old young woman called Taneesha, who lived with her mother and sister, came to the first session in the company of her mother (who was unable to stay for the meeting at BRIEF due to her work commitments). Taneesha told me at the start of the session that her best hopes from the coaching would be that things went better in the family as she was arguing with the others and it wasn't a good time. I then moved, as usual, straight into the Tomorrow Question but even before I'd finished it Taneesha interrupted me to say 'The whole problem is me smoking weed'. So I began a discussion about what she was hoping from the work in relation to that and she said that 'I don't want to stop for definite, but I do want to cut back, because it's messing everything up'. So I simply incorporated that aspect of her 'preferred future' into the next day, and continued asking detailed questions about her life then. Taneesha was quite animated in discussing how life would be for her. If she woke up 'fresh, and not bare out of it' (her expression for the outcome of not using drugs) then she would get up earlier in the morning, she might talk more nicely to her sister and mother and would actually get to school on time rather than at 10.30 or 11 as she usually did. The description carried on through the day and included references to her friends, both those who used drugs and those who didn't, and how she and they would like relationships to be. Eventually I asked her where on a scale she would put things now and she said '3'.

Coach: How come you're at 3 and not 0?

Taneesha: I'm not in prison! And they didn't kick me out from school. That's two main points. And I didn't lose everyone because of it. Well, I kind of did my family.

Coach: So you kind of lost your family in this process but not completely, because your mother was here, I met her when you arrived, she came with you so she's hanging in there with you, is that fair?

It's usually a mistake to try to encourage clients to 'see the positives'.

Taneesha: No, she only came because she thought I wouldn't come. It's not about her caring about me it's just about her controlling me 'cos she doesn't believe me.

Coach: So that's not the way you want it to be. You don't want her distrusting you. So you feel that when you look at how you got to 3, you haven't lost all your family, so how are you keeping your relationships going?

Taneesha: I try and be good from time to time.

Coach: Tell me about that.

Taneesha: It's so complicated. I try to be good for myself but the other reason I want to be good is because I want to get something . . .

. . . and here Taneesha described how her mother offers to take her shopping if she 'obeys the rules' but as soon as she's bad she doesn't get the shopping, and even when she does get the shopping she wonders if 'I'm only doing it for the stupid shopping' rather than for herself. In other words, she described very succinctly the dilemma of the typical teenager!

Coach: Can you think of a time recently when you were really doing it for yourself and not for the reward?

Taneesha: I don't get it anyway! I try to be good for some time but I just can't do it, I have to go out or whatever and if I go out then obviously I'm late and then she's getting pissed off and says 'you ain't getting it no more, I told you the rules' and I get pissed off and we're arguing and then I leave the house . . .

. . . and off she went, describing graphically the pattern of problematic interaction with her mother. I tried again.

Coach: So when was the last good day? You say there are days when you make an effort and it is a good day, give me an example of that.

Taneesha: I don't know. I can't remember. That's one of the things when you blaze a lot, you don't remember the days.

By now I had had it explained to me that 'blaze' was the street term for smoking weed and had nothing to do with having blazing rows with people, and I did not let this diversion throw me off course!

Coach: Even if you can't pinpoint it, think back to a day . . .

Taneesha: Well, it depends how much sleep I got, or even if I got any, and I wake up fresh, and my sister's not shouting at me (*earlier she had said her sister shouted at her to get up and go to school*) then I'm happy. And if people piss me off at school . . .

Coach (*interrupting*): OK, so there are lots of things that can happen during the day that can trip you up. If I can take you back to the 3 on the scale (*and here I summarised what she had told me so far, starting with not being in prison)* . . .

Taneesha: Well, people don't think I'm a crackhead.

Coach: What's their evidence for that?

Taneesha: I still take care of myself . . .

She talked about taking care of her appearance and trying to 'look fresh'.

Coach: Wow, this is terrific stuff, I'm trying to get a note of it. I'm writing things down here. I want to hear 20 things that tell you you're at 3 on the scale. I've probably got 7 or 8 things so far, and I want to keep on writing.

Taneesha: *20* things?

Coach: Yes. Let's see how many we've got so far (*here I summarised the list and it was 7*). So let's keep going.

Taneesha (*putting her head on her hand*): What else can I think of? Hmm. Like, if I meet new people they don't think I'm so bad, even if I'm in bare trouble I don't show it, even if I'm pissed off I put a smile on my face.

Coach: How do you do that? How come if you're in bare trouble you don't show it?

Taneesha: I just have to do it, don't I, because, one, I don't want to worry her, and two, I don't know, I just want to forget about it . . .

Coach: OK, I'm writing down here 'I don't want to worry her'.

Asking for a list of 20 things might have seemed a gamble on my part but an SF coach who knows about the power of the 'what else?' question has no qualms in challenging his or her clients to dig deep. If I had truly felt that she might not have got to this number then I would have given a lower figure so as to avoid short-changing her; however, one doesn't want to give too low a figure either! On one occasion I asked a 16-year-old young man with Asperger's syndrome to find ten things he'd noticed had been better since the previous meeting and he thought he would never get that many and I kept going until I had 12 things. At the next meeting, the young man said he'd had a bad week but said 'are we going to do those ten things again?' and naturally I complied, and even though on this occasion we could only get to seven things, this brought a big smile to his face and was better than the two or three things he might only have managed if he hadn't been aiming at a bigger list.

The second session with Taneesha began rather oddly. I asked her 'What's been better since we met a week ago?' and she said 'Nothing really'. Undeterred, I asked her to think back to the days immediately after we met. I was working on the principle that clients often – in most cases, in fact – make progress immediately after a session but then begin to slip back. Taneesha said 'I tried to be good for a day, but then things got bad again'. I was about to ask her about how, at least, she had managed to *try* to be good for a day when she added, with a mysterious air, 'and today's the third day'. I waited but she didn't say anything more. 'Third day of . . .?' 'Not blazing!' she said with a smile. The smile reassured me that this was good news to her and not just me, and asked her a number of questions about what she had done on the days she hadn't 'blazed'. As she talked she looked more and more pleased with herself and then I shook her hand in congratulation.

There are times with clients who misuse drugs and alcohol when it is useful to ask them 'How did you resist the urge to use?' a question that the Milwaukee group originally devised. In the case of Taneesha this didn't seem necessary because she was able to identify clearly what she had done differently on the days she didn't use. She had jumped up her scale (to 7). In the next session she had continued to make progress and she felt family relationships had vastly improved.

Working with bereaved clients

Occasionally a coach may receive a referral of a young person who has recently been bereaved, or has experienced loss between sessions.

Bereavement is not a 'problem' to be solved. It is part of life and has to be endured as such. This means that first and foremost the coach will seek to listen to whatever it is the young person wants to say about what they are going through. If this means that they wish to talk at length about difficulties and pain, then it is not being 'problem focused' to let them do that. We can ask them what they are hoping to talk about in our meeting. It is quite common to find that a young person is quite clear that they *don't* want to talk about what happened, and to insist that this be the focus of the work (together with the more traditional counselling approach of asking how they are 'feeling') is unhelpful. Even when they are prepared to talk about the events surrounding their loss, they often say that what they are hoping for from the coaching relates to moving forward in their lives. One 15-year-old, whose father had died 3 weeks before, said that his best hopes from our work were to improve his confidence. We explored what difference that would make to his life and what was helping him achieve that in future. He said that his father had been keen for him to succeed and he wanted to show him he could do it. Another young man, 12 years old, who lost his mother 3 months before to cancer, and then received news of the death of a cousin 2 days before our session, talked about wanting to be more confident at school and to reduce the number of detentions he had been receiving.

If the client does want to talk about what they are going through then the emphasis is on how they are *coping* with things. Sessions with one 16-year-old who suffered the calamity of losing both his parents within a few months of each other (as the one was dying of cancer, the other suffered a fatal heart attack), looked at how he was managing, where he got his support from, how he succeeded into getting into school when he could (he slept badly and mornings were very difficult for him), and how he was managing his understandable anger at people (such as doctors) he felt had let his family down. He was occasionally asked to reflect upon what he thought his parents would have been most pleased to have seen him doing in relation to trying to continue with his education and in his consideration towards other family members.

Last but not least: how to keep their attention

Adolescents can be quite variable, and while there are times when they converse in a totally adult manner, there are also occasions when coaches can feel like they are talking to a young child. The conversation can be moving along nicely and suddenly a look comes over the young person and they start to yawn, look away, fidget and so on. There is no magic answer in these situations. There will be times when the coach will even decide to ignore the behaviour altogether on the grounds that as long as the client is *answering* the questions then it is not for us to judge whether they are engaged or not. I once carried out a 'conversation' with one young man who spent the whole time walking about the room, kicking a paper football around. On other occasions it is necessary to ask directly whether they want to continue the session, or whether they are listening at all. One time I could hear the sound of music coming from the headphones that the boy was wearing. When I asked him if he wouldn't mind turning his music off he said 'what music?' I said I thought I could hear it coming from his headphones. He paused, listened intently and said with apparent surprise, 'oh yes!' and turned his machine off.

The coach's decision about how to handle these situations will be influenced by the degree of their own tolerance for certain behaviours. Working with one young woman I noticed that she started to yawn and look away, and although she was still answering questions her replies were getting increasingly shorter and so I decided to try to vary my questions. I engaged in a spot of 'SF self-supervision', asking myself what questions I could ask her that might be different enough to engage her, and came up with a scale question, which thankfully had the desired effect. But it doesn't always 'work' and there have been times when I've called the session to an early halt because it seems we are no longer doing any useful work. And the evidence from follow up suggests that progress can still be made and the actual length of the session seems immaterial.

Perhaps the most important lesson to be learned in talking to young people is to listen, and to look for signs of their creativity at work. One young man was telling me about the progress he was making in getting up earlier in the mornings. 'How have you done that?' 'I've set my alarm on my phone with a song I don't like.'

Reference

Berg, I.K. and Steiner, T. (2003) *Children's Solution Work*. New York: W.W. Norton.

Chapter 4

Parents

Taking an interactional view

One of the major influences on the development of SF practice was that of systems thinking, especially the idea that change in one part of a system will lead to change in other parts. Family therapy grew out of this and developed the idea that where a child or a young person was the 'identified patient' it would be productive to meet with members of their family. Some therapists went as far as to insist that the *whole* family attend for therapy. Though SF coaches do not use systems theory as an explanation of human behaviour, they have made great use of its more practical application, the hard-to-argue-against idea that our behaviour affects and influences those around us. This is why it is not unusual for parents to report improvements in their child's behaviour at home, even when the coach has only been focusing on behaviour at school – an improvement in one area of life will almost certainly have a knock-on effect on other seemingly unrelated areas of life. The practical value of this is that we can work with parents or teachers even though the child refuses to attend. As it is usually adults, whether parents, teachers or other professionals, who want the child or young person to change, it is not uncommon for young people, particularly teenagers, to refuse to go along with the plan. Once we accept the strength of mutual influence within families and within schools, the child's actual presence in a coaching session is no longer as necessary as it would seem.

The SF coach therefore takes an interactional view. If a young person is complaining about her parents because they are telling her she can't stay out beyond a certain time we will resist the urge to ask her to compromise or to ask her why she doesn't comply. Instead, we will ask her what difference it would make if she were allowed to stay out to the time she wants. This is not because we necessarily support her behaviour but rather because we are hoping to find a route to a description of how she and her parents might relate if the conflict were resolved. She might talk about being happier. Then we would begin to develop the interactional line of questioning by asking her how her parents would know she was happier, what the effect would be on them from knowing that – the change in their behaviour – and how she would respond to their change of behaviour. She might say that instead of lots of rows going on there would be talking and shared activities. We would aim for a detailed description of the interactional aspects of behaviour, to create chains of influence. If we are talking to the parent who was complaining about their daughter staying out late, we would follow the same line of questioning: if she came home at the time they wanted her to, what difference would that make to them? How would she know that? How might she respond and how might they respond to her? We would probably find that we ended up at the same place, where they were saying that there would be talking rather than rows, and so on. One of the advantages of this way of working is that even when it seems that one party is complaining about another, as in these examples, the outcome is that the complainer becomes included in the solution. It is important that coaches do not allow themselves to get caught up in the detail about things, such as what time the young person will come home, as this is at the very heart of the battleground and there's no easy way out. Instead, the coach is thinking outside of the box of that conflict, and looking at its resolution. If as a result of the coaching the relationship between parents and child improves then it is likely that they will work out their own resolution to the timekeeping conflict.

Sandra and Tracey

It is probably the most commonly asked question in relation to work with parents and their offspring: how can their frequently opposing wishes be reconciled? An example of this concerned a social services referral of a worrying case where Tracey, aged 15, was being repeatedly accommodated by the local authority. She didn't get on with her mother or her mother's boyfriend, and things would reach a pitch whereby she would run away from home. After a few days she would show up at her father's place and stay with him until they argued and she would run away again. Finally, the police would be called and she would go to a foster home before returning to her mother's, and then the cycle would repeat itself.

Tracey came with her mother, Sandra, and the problems between them were being aired even before they sat down. Sandra was complaining about Tracey's refusal to go to school, and about how much time she was spending with her older, unemployed boyfriend (social workers had investigated the nature of this relationship). When I asked the Miracle Question, Sandra described how Tracey would come down for breakfast at 7.30 with her school uniform on; immediately Tracey started interrupting. Such interruptions are not uncommon, especially at the start of a session when clients are still in 'argumentative' mode. And we do our best to ignore them. Continuing, I encouraged Sandra to talk about what would be different after Tracey returned from school. She spoke about how they would spend quality time together, talking, watching TV and going out shopping. After about 10 minutes I turned to Tracey and asked what her 'Miracle' day would look like. She started by saying she'd get up at 10 o'clock at which point it was Sandra's turn to interrupt. Again, I persevered and encouraged Tracey to say what would be happening between her and her mother at that time and she said she would make her mother a cup of tea and they would have a cigarette together and talk and then they would go shopping. As I had anticipated, their descriptions of a better future began to overlap and a very different atmosphere was being generated in the room. There was much that they loved and appreciated about each other but had 'forgotten' in the heat of their conflict. The more these positive aspects of their relationship were brought back into view the more likely they were to find their own way to settle arguments.

This is one of the keys to SFBC: focusing towards the positive aspects of a relationship, both in the past and the future, is likely to be more effective than trying to negotiate through the conflict. By building up the relationship we are helping parent and child to find the wherewithal to make their own way through the difficulty. With Sandra and Tracey, I was sympathetic to the mother's concerns and her wish for my support while at the same time keeping out of the dispute. By concentrating on the possibilities within their relationship my intention was that they would find their own resolution.

Sandra and Tracey asked for follow-up appointments, but for different reasons (usually the sickness of one or the other) they did not attend. Sandra was consistently positive about their experience of the first session and I learned from the social worker that mother and daughter were getting on much better. Although Tracey did not return to school she started going to college. About 3 or 4 months later Sandra called to ask me to see Tracey on her own because she was worried that her daughter was going to give up college due to pressure from her boyfriend. Tracey agreed to see me but by then she had made up her mind. We tried looking at how she might find a 'third way' which would allow her to stay in college without upsetting her boyfriend but it led nowhere, as her confidence (rated on a scale) that she could go to college *and* keep the relationship was very low. Her commitment (again, rated on a scale) to keeping the relationship was markedly higher than that of continuing to go to college. I then switched to asking about her hopes for the future given this new direction. She talked of getting a job and finding a way to manage her boyfriend's distrust.

With Tracey's permission I called Sandra and talked about the meeting we'd had. Two months later Sandra called to tell me that Tracey had left college. However, she had got a job (she was now 16) and she, Sandra, was very pleased with the sense of responsibility that Tracey was showing. It wasn't quite what she'd been hoping for Tracey, but it was 'good enough'. The relationship between mother and daughter remained firm and she never ran away from home again.

Working with the parent alone

When a parent asks for help with their child they often hope or even expect that the coach will work with the child alone. Where this proves impossible (the child refusing to be seen alone, for example), or is ineffective, the coach may engage with both the parent and the child. Or, they may choose to see the parent alone, as part of an overall strategy for helping the child.

In another situation, a parent may specifically request help around an aspect of their parenting because of an issue that has arisen at a particular time (such as bereavement, or marital breakdown), or in relation to general parenting areas (such as getting young children to stay in their beds or dealing with teenagers). Coaching skills are invaluable in helping parents to develop ideas about the kind of family life they want and ways to create that.

Gemma

Gemma wanted help for Jane, her 15-year-old daughter, who had suddenly stopped going to school. She arrived for the first meeting at BRIEF distressed because Jane was refusing to leave the car. We discussed options, and Gemma tried once again to persuade Jane to join us. She still refused but said she would wait in the car while her mother and I talked.

When asked what her hopes from the coaching were, Gemma said that she wanted 'to get ideas on how to support Jane so that she can get back into school and do her exams'. I asked her what signs she was already seeing that gave her hope that Jane would manage this. After reflecting on this question Gemma came up with three significant pointers. Firstly, Jane had shown interest in what was said at the parents' evening at the school a few days before; secondly, Jane was saying that she felt she would be able to catch up with the missed work; and, thirdly, Jane was still seeing her school friends.

This led into future-focused questions, and Gemma talked about how her daughter would be starting the day, the sorts of things she would be saying about school (for example, a willingness to discuss future subject choices without closing down the conversation), and generally being in what she called 'school mode'. When we looked again for signs of this already happening it turned out that Jane had begun to get up earlier in the day and wasn't just pulling the covers over her head.

It is readily apparent that the dominant theme here was of Gemma talking about what she wanted to see *Jane* doing. This can be helpful in itself as the parent might then be more likely to notice any changes in the daughter's behaviour. But we can go further, and taking an interactional view we can ask the parent to reflect on their *responses* to the changed behaviour of the young person. With this in mind, I enquired as to how the parents would be responding to signs of progress in future as well as to the progress they were already seeing. When discussing how Jane might be talking about her school work, Gemma remembered that Jane had accused her of asking 'embarrassing questions' and she began to think about how she might talk to Jane in future in a way that was supportive rather than worrying her and pressurising her. The signs of hope she was seeing in Jane enabled her to feel that she could afford to step back a little and she intended to find ways to help her husband do similarly – for example, to encourage him not to go into Jane's room in the mornings when she wasn't getting up at a 'decent' time.

Engaging the parent with the young person

Ann and Patrick

There are times when the coach might make the decision to try to engage the parent of a young person they are seeing and this occurred with Patrick, a 14-year-old student who was being coached in school. After eight sessions I was feeling stuck. The young man was sometimes making progress, but each time it seemed the work could end there were setbacks leading to more appointments being set up for him. He seemed to act as a class clown to gain the attention of his peers, and frequently said outrageous things out loud that led to teachers having to send him out of the lesson. In brief coaching, the question of how to progress in what looks like an unchanging situation is one that we have to address. We do not think it is sufficient to go on and on working with someone without having a sense that some lasting change is being achieved. The question of 'What can I do differently?' arises and one possibility is to involve a 'significant other', someone who has some influence over the client. This might be another professional in the school, a member of the peer group or a parent. In Patrick's case, with his agreement, a meeting was set up with his mother, Ann. After a few minutes, in which the reasons for the meeting were discussed with her, we focused on Ann's concern that her son make good choices about who are good friends for him to associate with, how to say no to people, and how he can earn rewards from his mother for doing so, something that interested Patrick immensely.

If Patrick had not been present, I would have aimed to develop the same sort of conversation as in the case of Gemma and Jane. However, in this case I was able to ask him to respond to his mother's ideas of what he could do to thrive in school and to not get into trouble. When his responses became vague I encouraged Ann to probe for more detail rather than doing the questioning myself. I was also able to encourage conversation between them about instances of success in the past. She talked about the ability her son had shown while at primary school to make good friends, which led to the two discussing how he'd done that and how she had helped him in the past.

Summary

- Even where the young person is seen as the person who needs to change, it is possible to do successful work with someone significant in their life, such as a parent, without the son or daughter even being present.
- Parents care about their children and are keen to see them make changes so that their lives, and the life of the family, will go better. The SF coach will focus on the positive *consequences* of these changes rather than the changes themselves. A focus on envisaging the life they want offers them opportunities to move towards it.
- In looking at the consequences of change, it is constructive to use interactional sequences of questions that highlight changes to the *relationship* between the family members.

Chapter 5

Groupwork

Groupwork is an important mode of working with young people. Partly it's a matter of convenience: in a setting such as a school, it provides a way to work with several young people at once. It is a way to impact on the peer group, and so, in some areas of work, for example with gangs, it avoids targeting particular individuals as being in need of 'help'. There is also the usefulness of giving individuals the opportunity to learn from, and to contribute to, the others in the group. Even when every participant's issues are different there is a sense of group identity that can be mutually empowering for the members.

Several books on SF groupwork are now available and we particularly recommend the work of John Sharry and Linda Metcalf (Sharry 2007; Metcalf 1998).

Setting up the group

Getting a group going is often the biggest challenge in groupwork. In certain settings, such as a school or youth offending teams, the young people may have relatively little choice about attending. In other contexts, such as youth clubs and voluntary agencies, there is always the question about how to engage potential group participants. It is extremely frustrating to spend time and energy finding premises for the group, networking and setting things up, to find that only two or three people appear.

There is a considerable list of items that the facilitator might have to bear in mind even before the group starts. First and foremost is the question of who the group is for and how many will attend; when and where and for how long it will be held and how long each session will be; and how clients will be recruited. Even the question of the name can be crucial. We were asked to run an 'anger management' group for six year-9 boys (age 14) in an inner city school, and when I asked them if they were happy to tell their friends they were coming to a group with that name they of course said 'no' and there ensued a lengthy discussion about the name they wanted for *their* group (they decided that 'Solutions For A Change' was best for them; a name I heartily approved of!). Then there is the question of how group members will be chosen; for example, each potential client can be interviewed separately to ensure that they understand what the group is about and that it is right for them. Co-workers (most groups are co-led) will need to decide whether they are running an open or closed group: with young people it is likely to be a closed group that they have to sign up for in its entirety – but in some contexts an open-door might seem reasonable, especially as new people get the word and become interested. In addition, there is the question of whether the group is single-sex or mixed. There are also questions related to what might happen both before the session (where will people gather?) and immediately after, and about confidentiality, a very important issue as far as young people are concerned. None of these questions is, in itself, in any way related to SF practice; these are just the questions that every group facilitator has to take account of right from the start.

An example of where planning in advance was essential relates to when I was asked to work in a youth club with a group of young men who were members of gangs and were becoming increasingly involved in crime. I was told that as many as 15 adolescents would be likely to attend the group. The group had been on a residential weekend in which they had experienced intensive workshops in relation to resolving conflict, keeping safe, choices and consequences, status and revenge. The hope was that the subsequent groupwork of three meetings with me as an external coach would help to ensure that the youths concerned would retain the learning from the residential weekend 2 months previously. We scheduled a week between the first and second meetings and a longer gap to the third meeting.

There was the option of seeing all the young people in one large group but I considered the possibility of this being a format that would be harder for participants to engage with for any length of a time and decided instead to put them into groups of three and to have 15–20 minutes with each group. I believed that this would increase the chance that they would be focused and productive. The young people were playing pool in the club, and when their turn came they made their way to the room especially set aside for the sessions. The total groupwork time amounted to one and a half hours, and even with the assistance of a youth worker from the centre as co-worker, it was fairly exhausting work. The young men had been offered the inducement of going go-karting at the end if they attended all the sessions and attendance was close to 100%! Because of this, it was mostly possible to keep the groups the same.

It is important to consider what kind of 'ground rules' there should be in the group, and as much as possible it is advisable to create these rules with the group members themselves. When young people are asked 'How will we know we're working well together?' they will, in most cases, come up with good ideas regarding 'showing respect', punctuality, and so forth. If the group coach thinks that something important is being missed, then they can work this into the discussion by saying, for example, 'If we're working well together and someone's mobile phone rings, how would we deal with it?'.

Again, these are not SF considerations in themselves, but if clarified in advance with the young people then this will make the job a lot easier. If an attendee is persistently late, or constantly talking over others, then the simplest place to start in dealing with it is from the previously agreed upon ground rules for participating in the group.

The first group session

Groupwork cannot be tightly fitted into a formal structure because the coach has to be responsive to events as they happen, and groupwork with young people can be extremely unpredictable. However, we have found that it is still possible to create a flexible enough template to work from.

The usual starting point for an SF session is to ask the client what their best hopes are from attending, and it follows that the ideal start to groupwork is to invite each person in turn to tell the group what they are hoping the group sessions will lead to for them. However, immediately we run into the ways in which groupwork makes us adapt our practice. For example, if there has been no prior introductory meeting with each individual member, then the very act of asking people to introduce themselves needs to be considered carefully. In our experience, simply asking people to say who they are can lead to some trying to be helpful in providing information that hasn't been requested (about their particular problems, for example). We have learned to begin the first group with a more specific, and SF, suggestion. For example, 'I'd like you to introduce yourselves to the group by telling us your name and something that has gone well in your life in the last week'.

After introductions, the SF coach will usually want to move into future-focused questions, beginning by asking to hear the best hopes that each person has for themselves from the programme. This is true of all groupwork but particularly so in groups where someone (a teacher, say) has defined in advance what the group is 'about'. In the first session the aim is to enable the participants to establish their own 'personal' contract for being in the group. Teri Pichot suggests that the coach should aim to have everyone decide on a group 'theme', an aim for the future that all can share (Pichot with Smock 2009). This has the value of giving the coach a keyword or phrase that stands for everyone's aims.

The structure of a first session in groupwork could follow the individual format:

* Best hopes from attending the group sessions
* Preferred future: what their lives will be like when they've achieved those hopes
* Instances of the preferred future already happening
* Exceptions to problem behaviour
* Scale to measure each person's progress
* Ending with compliments

An aspect of groupwork that the coach will have to consider is the attention span of the young people present. This will have been taken into account in deciding on the length of a group session and the number of young people present. In the example of the anger management group, the time allocated to each meeting was 45 minutes and it quickly became apparent to me that this was a *very* long time indeed for these young men. After a chaotic first meeting my strategy was to arm myself at the next meeting with a supermarket bag full of food and drink. If there's one law about young adolescent males it's that they are nearly always hungry so I instituted a 'tuck break' in the middle of the session, during which I produced some simple – and healthy – eats and drinks, and the increasingly fractious group was suddenly reduced to happy sounds of munching and slurping and were more relaxed for the second half of the meeting. I timed the break to come after exploring progress that they had made in the last week, and before moving on to explore signs of making further progress in the week to the next meeting.

Subsequent meetings

The task of the coach in later meetings is to do a detailed follow-up on whatever progress has been made and, in the case of setbacks, how the clients have coped with them and how they have managed to get back on track – or, how they will know they will be back on track. It is important for the coach to remember that this is not about checking up whether the clients have managed to do any of the things they indicated might be signs of progress, and it *is* about looking for all and any signs of progress and not just those relating to the preferred outcomes.

As in individual work, the structure of follow-up sessions is as follows:

- What's better? Exploring progress since the previous meeting
- If there have been setbacks, then exploring how they have coped
- Use of scale questions to ascertain the degree of progress made
- Signs of progress that could be looked out for until the next meeting
- Ending with compliments

Group example: working in a school

The example that follows is taken from a group of eight 14-year-old boys in school that I was asked to meet together with their year head, Leo Beattie. We had planned a programme of seven sessions timed to end shortly before Progress Review Day (when students and their parents meet with the teachers). When we began to explore the students' preferred futures, we decided to use that as a target date.

Coach: I am going to ask each of you in turn to say what you are hoping to have achieved by the 15th December. We're going to go round the group one by one. If you can't think of anything to say, that's OK, you can say 'pass'.

The first boy said 'to improve my behaviour' and the second closely followed suit with 'improve my behaviour at school'. Leo had warned me that he was worried about 'students saying what they think I want to hear'. In SF we take clients seriously. One often hears responses that are surprisingly close to what the adults in their lives are hoping for and rather than distrusting them we see their hopes as doorways into more detailed explorations of the differences achieving these things would make. However, in groupwork one cannot do a separate interview with each client as one goes around the group, and so one has to learn to bide one's time. Things warmed up with the next boy (one can usually rely on competitiveness in groups of young men!): *Improve my behaviour in school and my learning. And I want to have high levels so my mum can be proud of me!*

I continued round the group, getting short statements from each student. At this stage I didn't ask questions about anybody's response except for one young man who talked about wanting 'to change my whole academic life, get experience and get my A Levels'. I praised his eagerness to look so far forward and asked him 'If you were moving *in the direction of* changing your academic life what would you notice yourself doing?'. He answered 'My grades going up'. The boy next to him talked about the need to 'go to sleep earlier' and the other boys giggled. This seemed an important moment. Firstly, no one would have predicted a comment like that in advance, and it shows the value of aiming to get individual hopes from young people. Secondly, when a response is as specific as this, it helps to ask extra questions such as 'What difference will that make?' in order to generalise further into the client's life. Thirdly, it raised the issue of how to limit disparaging comments or laughs from others, and at that point both Leo and I interjected with a compliment about the importance of getting more sleep. We were obviously concerned to limit any sniggering, although it would have been better for us to have checked with the group themselves what they thought about the importance of sleep, so that we weren't seen as becoming over-protective of one particular student.

Leo told the group that he was hearing things about the boys that he didn't know – and wouldn't have predicted. So we went round a second time, getting everyone to share further signs of progress from their point of view; the answers included doing revision at home, getting to school on time, getting off report cards, and so on.

Then, as a variation – and to ensure that they stayed attentive – I introduced for the third round the following question:

'What do you hope by December 15th *other students* will notice different about you?'

The first student in line seemed stumped by this question (or maybe he wasn't paying attention) and couldn't answer, so I suggested that he take time to think about it and moved on to the next student, Jason, who said 'They'll be able to think that I've become more intelligent'.

Coach: Good. And how would they know that?
Jason (shrugs): Umm . . . don't know.
Coach: What would tell them you were more intelligent?
Jason (further shrug): Don't know.
Coach: They can't see inside your head, so what is it you'd be doing that would tell them that?
Jason: Getting everything right!

By the time we had gone round the group, the first student was able to answer the question. There was no time for more in that first meeting, which lasted only 30 minutes.

We began the second session by asking each student what progress they had made, and made several rounds of the group in a similar fashion to the first meeting: things they had noticed about themselves and what they thought others had noticed about them. We then did a round of 'If next week things are progressing, what would you be most pleased to notice?'. The third meeting began in exactly the same way as before – 'What progress have you made since last week, what's been good for you?'– and we stayed with the format of moving round the group sequentially. Occasionally a boy would be unable to answer and he would be allowed to 'pass'; whenever that happened, he was then able to give an answer when the group came back round to him again. During this particular session, instead of a round of questions about signs of progress to come, Leo wondered whether the boys would like to hear what he had noticed in the school and I said it would be useful to go round and have each of them say what they *thought* he was going to say he had noticed about them, and then later he added his observations. Although this meant there wasn't time to ask about signs of progress to come in the next week, it gave everyone the opportunity to hear about the very good progress that all the boys were making.

During the third session a boy arrived late, and when it came to his turn to answer he said 'What are we talking about?' and I took this opportunity to ask for a volunteer to explain exactly that. Inevitably there were moments of indiscipline, and Leo said he'd found that he'd had to give a couple of boys what he called the 'death stare' when they were starting to giggle!

Before the fourth meeting, Leo and I discussed the idea of varying the way we were running the group, not because what we were doing wasn't working, but simply to ensure variety and also to fit with his more dynamic style. Leo therefore took the reins and he had a great idea for getting the boys more involved with talking to each other:

Leo: I'm going to kick off today. You all identified things you wanted to achieve by December. Now I'm presuming, and I know from walking around the school, that you guys have done a lot of that stuff already. What I'd like you to do is a timed exercise of 30 seconds. I want you to turn to your partner (*and here Leo pointed out the pairs who would be working together*) and you've got 30 seconds to tell them as many things as you can about what you've been doing differently, and I want you to explain how you've been doing them, since we started doing this group. *What* you've been doing, and *how* you've been doing them.

The exercise consisted of one person telling the other what they had managed to do, and after Leo had called time they switched round. At the end he asked each person to share with the group what they had learned from their partner. I was impressed at how much they had managed to learn about their partners in a short time.

In the fifth session, he encouraged them to talk about their 'dreams' – 'Where would you hope to be in 5 years' time?'. One bright spark said 'I can't think ahead. I could get run over!' At which I asked '*suppose* you make it through' and then he was able to answer. We then introduced scale questions for the first time (rather late in the day!), and asked them to think of how far they were in relation to achieving their 'dreams'. We emphasised the importance of exploring as much as possible about how they had got to where they were before moving on to thinking about signs of moving up their scale.

In the sixth session, we started with the question 'What's better?'. All of the boys were continuing to make progress, so having reminded them that there was only one further meeting to go after this one, we asked them how they would know that the time remaining was useful to them. We wanted to check if there was anything new or different that we may have missed, and the boys reiterated most of the same wishes in relation to academic levels and to behaviour.

One boy referred to not wanting people to laugh at him. 'How would you like it to be?' He answered 'People to take me more seriously'. We asked him a number of questions about what people would do and how he would respond. The group joined in with advice, for example, telling him he needed to smile less and look at people more. Even Leo found it hard to resist saying that 'from a teacher's point of view' it would help him if he remembered to take his coat off! We acknowledged that there was quite a lot of pressure being put on the student and asked him to reflect on what he'd heard that was potentially most useful to him, and he mentioned looking differently at people and not laughing when they laughed.

Among other topics that were discussed was, much to my surprise, that of improving reading skills. I told them how impressed I was, because in my experience boys are often reluctant to be seen reading, and as this discussion grew one of the boys opened his bag and produced a book he was reading and another boy talked about working in the library. I asked them what the benefits were to getting more reading done, and ways to achieve that.

At the end of this meeting Leo congratulated the boys on how hard they had worked for each other and how much they had used their brains, adding that he'd enjoyed this meeting the most.

Session 7, the last, was a treat for the boys because also present that day was Cynthia Franklin, Professor of Social Work at the University of Texas in Austin, who was in London to give a presentation for BRIEF. As an author of many research articles and books on SF practice, including a book on SF work in schools (Kelly et al 2008), I knew she would enjoy the chance to sit in with a group of students in a British school. Several of the boys said beforehand how pleased they were to be meeting her ('I've never met a professor before!'), especially as none of them had ever spoken to a Texan. At the end of the meeting she said that she wondered if they had expected her to arrive on a horse wearing a hat!

Leo began the meeting by showing the boys a segment of the tape from the first meeting in which they had talked about their hopes of what they wanted to achieve by the Progress Review day. We then did rounds on 'What are you already doing to move towards achieving what you want to achieve?'; I urged them to think of other things they had achieved, not only what they'd heard themselves say on the tape, and this helped to elicit a range of unexpected answers, such as one boy saying he'd been working on not being lazy, something we'd not heard from him before. We then suggested introducing a progress scale, and Cynthia accepted our invitation to take over this line of questioning. She set a scale 'where 0 means you haven't made any progress at all, which I know does not apply to anyone here, and 10 is you've got as far as you can get', and she went carefully round the group, patiently drawing out each boy in terms of their scale rating (the range was 6 to 8) and the progress they had made, with questions like 'How do you think you did that?' and asked them questions about what it was about the group that helped them. She then moved on to questions about moving up their scales: for example, 'If you could change your effort in some way, what would you see yourself doing? How would you know you were concentrating?'. One boy said he didn't think anyone could be a 10 and she agreed with him: 'There's always something to work on' which inspired her to ask another scaling question: 'How confident are you of keeping your progress, even past the Review day and the holidays into the new year?' (they all said 7!). Given this was the last meeting, this was an excellent way to help the boys to think further forward, and she emphasised how the group had helped each other so far and asked them how they could continue to do that in future.

As an end note, I'd like to add this interesting interchange that occurred in the fifth session when a boy suddenly popped a challenging question:

Jason: Why are we doing this?
Leo: Excellent question! Anyone got any answers?
Tuhin: To show people something.
Leo: Show them what, for example?
Tuhin: That anyone can change.
Leo: Ahmed, what were you going to say? (*as Ahmed had spoken at the same time as Tuhin*)

Ahmed: I was going to say the same thing.

Leo: OK. Nahid, why do you think we're doing this?

Nahid: I think when we finish this we can look back and think about what we used to do bad in school and then we can see that we can do work more seriously and stuff. You can see how you've changed.

Leo: That's really interesting.

Harvey: I agree, and it's such a good question that I'm wondering about what people think about doing this as a group, rather than talking separately. What's the advantage of everyone being in the room together talking like this?

Jordan: Because if everyone's in a group, they can express their feelings in front of their friends; if it's true, your friends can agree with you but if you do it by yourself you don't know what to say sometimes.

Jason: Because if we didn't do this, everyone would just be bad.

Leo: So you're saying if we hadn't done this everyone would have been bad?

Jason: Yeah.

Leo: Would they?

Jason: Yeah. Because when we first came here everyone was bad.

Leo: You feel you've made progress coming here?

Jason: Yeah.

Lessons from groups

When doing groupwork one quickly learns that it is not possible to dwell for long on each person's responses. This is possible to some extent with adult groups, but with young people it is vital to keep things moving along so that no one feels bored or, worse still, left out. At one point I said, with some frustration, 'gosh, there's so much more I would like to ask you about that but I have to move on to the next person'. The coach can feel that they are depriving the young person of the chance for a more in-depth SF exploration of their preferred future or success. However, the experience of this group, and of others, is that it works, and this teaches us something about how constructive the group experience can be for participants. The answers they give might be short, but the thinking they put into them is long, given the time they have to consider their answers as they await their turn. In other words, the participants are 'working' even when the spotlight is on someone else; and even if they are not, even if they have 'tuned out' while others are talking, they will begin to construct a useful answer the moment they begin to open their mouths. Of course, it helps to arrange to vary the questions and find ones that they weren't expecting (such as 'What will your friends notice you doing when you arrive at school?') in order to keep them on their toes. Perhaps the most important lesson here is that while we should aim to be as inclusive as possible, we don't have to strive to 'equalise air time': participants will talk for varying amounts of time but even those who hardly say a word (or 'pass' a lot) can be assumed to be working and learning.

We can't know in advance with absolute certainty what a young person is going to say, and one of the wonderful lessons from groupwork is how creative they can be. We need to listen out for the wisdom of individual members, which we can then use rather than trying to be wise ourselves. For example, in one meeting of the anger-management group, a young man was saying how it was impossible for him to control himself when insulted by a student or teacher. An argument began, with others telling him that he could control it and him digging his heels in further and further. A boy in the group then said 'If I had a million pounds to give you not to 'lose it', you wouldn't, would you?'. This was definitely a piece of 'local' wisdom that the whole group needed to ponder and discuss!

Another concern for facilitators is to what extent the coach should go round the group asking individual questions rather than asking people to talk to each other. This is, perhaps, up to each coach to decide for themselves, and it was a useful lesson for me to watch how Leo set up his timed exercise. The difficulty of allowing people to start talking to each other is that the coach has to cede control of the interactions, and while it can be productive in some situations it can also lead in a non-constructive direction. For example, one thing we have learned is the importance of emphasising to groups that people should avoid telling others what they should do. Young people – like adults, of course – are only too keen to show off their greater 'expertise' and what happens frequently to the recipient of this advice is that they argue back, usually starting with the immortal words 'yes, but . . .'. It isn't always like this with young people, and there is often a chance that someone in the group has a really good idea that no-one else has thought of; however, we try to coach them in the art of asking each other useful questions. Scales are, inevitably, the easiest of the techniques they can adopt with each other.

How to keep the group varied and interesting

One of the difficulties the coach sometimes faces is how to make the group interesting and unpredictable so that the seemingly repetitive nature of the session does not alienate young people.

How the coach will want to do this will depend on their particular interests and also on what tools are available, especially in the case of primary-age children. For example, with younger children it is a good idea when using scale questions to have the children 'walk the scale', with numbers placed on sheets on the floor. Numbers can be replaced by anything that will capture the interest of young people, and there can be fun in deciding what will be on the scale, such as football teams or pop stars or even just colours. Drawing is always a good tool with younger children, and Carolyn Emanuel suggests that each child be asked to draw a Coat of Arms: they are given a large cardboard shield on which they can portray things they are good at, things they enjoy, a moment they have been proud of, and things they want to achieve in future; other children can be encouraged at the appropriate time to add to the shields of others (Emanuel 2005).

There is also the option of using role play. Our colleague Chris Iveson gives the following example from his work in a primary school – a story that also demonstrates the possibility of engaging young people in spontaneous groupwork when the time is right.

I was totally failing with Kamal, a 7-year-old on the edge of exclusion because of his aggressive behaviour. School and parents were at their wits' end, and after three sessions so was I. My fourth meeting was at the school, the plan being to see him with the deputy head, but as she was ill I was left in a corner of the school hall trying to engage a boy who was preferring to jump off the stage. It was desperation that drove me to his classroom. My failure to match the school's expectations had reduced my confidence to such an extent that when I tapped on the door I thoroughly expected to be told off. Instead, a very friendly teacher said hello to us both, and, when I made my request, responded not with outrage but with a delighted 'Of course!'. I asked to borrow six children.

All eight of us trotted back to the hall. 'I'd like you all to sit in a circle, please', I told the six volunteers, 'and I want you all to be very good and quiet children'. Immediately a perfect, crossed-legged knee-to-knee circle was formed, with Kamal and me on the outside. 'Now, Kamal', I said, 'I want you to ask to join the circle'. Wumph! And Kamal had crashed in knocking two of his classmates sideways and producing looks of horror and disapproval from the rest. 'Okay, let's have another go! Who would like to show how we join a circle nicely?' Seven hands immediately shot up. 'What's your name?' I asked a little girl opposite. 'Cecily', she said. 'Cecily, will you come and stand here and show us how to join a circle nicely.' Cecily stood on the edge of the circle and asked 'Please may I join the circle?'. No one moved, so I prompted a little: 'What do you say when Cecily asks nicely?'. 'Yes, you may!' chorused five voices. But there was still no room. 'And do you move a little bit to make space for Cecily?' 'Yes!' came the chorus, this time with six voices. 'Okay, Cecily, let's have another go – see if you can join the circle nicely.' Cecily took a deep breath and once again asked 'Please may I join the circle?'. Six angelic faces looked up at her and with their 'Yes you may' they shuffled round to make a space and Cecily sat down.

'Would someone else like to play Join the Circle?' Seven hands shot up, and thirteen goes later Kamal had twice 'joined the circle nicely'. What is more, his six classmates were so fulsomely appreciative of his 'nice' behaviour that he was positively glowing with pride. Feeling a little more confident now, we returned to the classroom and bravely asked Kamal's teacher if we could show the class our game. Along with his six new friends, Kamal for the third time demonstrated his new-found skill and I left him and his little group joining in a whole class game.

Kamal's parents rang a few days later to say that Kamal was now behaving himself and there was no need for him to be seen again.

(Iveson, personal communication)

Bill O'Hanlon is a good resource for creative ideas and one suggestion he has is of using simple stories to illustrate particular points: 'Metaphors and stories are indirect ways to communicate ideas. They involve talking about something that parallels or represents something else . . . We use them to give clients a tool kit of reassuring, encouraging and inspiring images that are easy to remember' (O'Hanlon & Beadle 1994: 43). In one group, I told the boys, when we were discussing the difficulties of containing one's anger, a teaching tale I had heard from O'Hanlon. The story is of a guru travelling with his disciples in India. The train is very crowded and at one point the guru goes off to get a drink and when he returns his seat has been taken by someone who pointedly looks away from him and refuses to move. The guru stands silently by the man, looking at him and waiting for him to move. The disciples watch with baited breath to see what will happen. The man continues to sit there. After a while, the guru suddenly starts shouting loudly at the man, telling him how he has no right to sit in someone else's seat, and after a few seconds the embarrassed man gets up and goes away and the guru resumes his seat and sits there as calmly as if nothing had happened. The disciples gather around, shocked by what they have seen. 'Master', they say, 'how come you lost your temper? You of all people!'. He looks at them in surprise. 'Lose my temper? No, I simply took anger out of my back pocket, used it and then put it back' (O'Hanlon 1995). Told with all the O'Hanlon story-telling skills I could muster, I managed to have the boys in the group hanging on my every word, and they gave feedback later as to how much they liked it. On another occasion I quoted to them an old Ethiopian saying I'd come across in an article: 'when the Grand Master passes, the wise peasant bows deeply and silently farts' (Wade 1997). Needless to say, this one went down particularly well.

I have told young people that they will receive a certificate of attendance at the end of the group and have asked them to write down what they thought or hoped would be written on the certificate about them. This relates to an intriguing technique that has been suggested (Campbell & Brasher 1994) whereby group leaders invite participants to anticipate what compliments they might receive from the leaders or others. The writers found that it led to others in the group challenging those who have particularly negative views of themselves, e.g. if one person said 'no-one will have anything nice to say about me because I know I've been a waste of space lately' then another participant may well challenge that view by referring to something constructive they'd heard them say.

Scale questions

Scales are invaluable techniques for young people – for measuring their progress – and can be used in a variety of creative ways to fit with what attendees are hoping to achieve in their lives.

Generally one would seek to introduce them as early as possible into the group sessions. For example, in the anger-management group I brought them in half way through the first meeting to explore their progress towards their different hoped-for futures, and in every subsequent meeting we began with where they had got to on their respective scales and what would be signs of further progress.

In the youth club work, because the sessions had been set up in advance to be a follow-up to their residential weekend, I had begun the first meeting by asking them 'What have you done since the weekend that shows you're making good use of it?'. Although I had been provided with information by the referrer about what had been covered during the weekend itself, I didn't mention these things or ask the young men about them. I took the view that *anything* they had done that they regarded as having been worthwhile was worthy of exploration. Responses ranged far and wide, to do with their peer group (there was almost no talk about 'gangs'), families and schools. I then asked them to scale their progress, with '10 = you've achieved everything you wanted from the weekend, and 0 = not achieved anything'. Their scores varied widely, ranging from 2 to 8, and I took an average for each group to create a sense of inclusiveness. The questions, as always for scales, were of two main categories: (1) How come you're at 'x' and not 0? and (2) How will you know you've reached +1? On one occasion a boy described having got involved in some gang violence since the previous session and rather than go over why that had happened, we focused on how he was now keeping himself safe (as he was fearful of repercussions) and how he now hoped to move forward.

It is helpful to avoid people having a sense of failure if they don't get to 10, and one way to achieve that is to ask people where on the scale they would be happy to get to (their 'good enough' point) while still striving to reach 10. For almost all clients the answer will be 7 or 8, in which case even reaching 'only' 5 or 6 would be seen by the group as making good progress.

Another example of a scale I have used is one where '10 = you are doing everything you can to achieve what you want to achieve, and 0 = you're doing nothing'. This is useful as a way of exploring and expanding on the client's commitment to change and it can be helpful to add questions about what significant others (including other members of the group) are seeing.

One issue that we have encountered has been what happens when a scale is first put to a group. In one group I worked with the first person to answer said '5', a not uncommon answer with adolescents. But subsequently everybody gave either 5 or above. There seemed to be some sort of competitive element at work (and these were all young men). I decided to ignore this. After all, it is not the number that is important so much as the detail that the client gives to justify the number; so whether they really thought that they were at 5, or would have said 3 if no one else was there to hear them, is probably of no importance.

Ending sessions

The usual SF practice is to summarise what clients have been saying but in the group context this is tricky, as it is hard to remember what everyone has said. With two workers it is possible for one to be taking notes, and for that person to summarise back to everyone, but it is still a laborious process for young people to have to endure. The simplest thing, then, is to give the group a general compliment – such as to comment on their thinking hard with you and then invite them to look out for progress over the following week. Another idea is to ask the young people to give each other compliments.

In the anger-management group I decided that, instead of complimenting the students, I'd ask *them* to compliment the group, and to comment on what they had found particularly interesting or enjoyable in the meeting that day. This latter idea also helped me to get feedback on what I could use more of in future, and in that way I learned that focusing on their achievements was important to them, that they liked the scale questions above all the other techniques I used, and the stories were appreciated. And I also got a list of what food items I needed to bring with me next time!

Ending the group

In individual work it is uncommon for the coach to know that it *is* the last session, because coaching should end as soon as it has fulfilled its purpose – which is usually between sessions. However, in groupwork, where the last session is usually known from the start, endings can be approached differently. The coach can start in the usual way by asking about progress since the last session, but the scale then used should specifically help to gauge the progress that people feel they have made in reaching the 'good enough' point they identified in session 1.

It isn't necessary to remind people what their original best hopes were; as in individual work, it is better for clients to have a sense of moving ahead in their lives rather than trying to achieve specific goals. However, this can be valuable with some, especially the younger age group.

As it is the last meeting, an opportunity could be provided for discussion about continuing to move forward in future as well as dealing with possible setbacks.

With younger children there may be the possibility of finishing the group in a more celebratory and ceremonial style. Certificates (nicely laminated if you can) of achievement are good for all ages, and younger children can also write on a card (or represent in drawings) what sort of things they hope to continue to do in future, and they can complete 'credit cards' to be given to those they feel have helped them along the way (Chapter 8). And then there will be a nice big cake to finish with!

There are various client-evaluation tools available that enable clients to both review their progress and give their views of how the group was for them. We have used the Outcome Rating Scales and Session Rating Scales devised by Scott Miller and colleagues; they have adapted their tools for use in groups (downloadable from Miller's website, scottdmiller.com). In addition, there is the possibility in some contexts of having the referrer attend the final group (even if only for the last 5 minutes) and to hear for themselves the progress clients have made.

In some cases a final, follow-up meeting might be arranged to review progress, but there are obvious practical difficulties in most circumstances. Establishing a way of getting feedback on outcomes, as in individual work, is useful, but in most cases the feedback is likely to be obtained in a spontaneous way. I learned from a member of staff for example, that of the six students in the anger-management group, four made good progress, one stayed the same, and one got worse. And in an inter-agency youth panel meeting that I was invited to attend with the worker from the youth club where we'd met with the gang-related youths, in which a Police Officer, Youth Offending Service worker, Housing Officer, Education Welfare Officer, Substance Misuse worker and Connexions worker were present, we learned about the considerable reduction of concerns people had about almost all the youths we'd worked with some months before.

Particular issues

Every single group throws up issues challenging to the coach, regardless of their model of practice. Groups for young people – and adults too – face the difficulty of those who are disruptive, either by talking too much or not at all, coming in late, messing about, rudeness, and, a particularly difficult issue in groups, of people laughing at someone for what they have said. There is no specific SF way of dealing with these things. One can either deal with them robustly (to the point of excluding someone from the group) or in a gentler fashion (including a separate talk outside of the group with the person concerned) but deal with it you must.

In a similar vein, there are issues that may have to be addressed head-on in a way that will take the coach away not just from SF coaching but from coaching generally. Confidentiality is important for everybody, and the coach may have to remind people of what the limits are to this, and particularly if they hear about something that they will have to take further, such as bullying and disclosures regarding violence, and threats of violence, at home or in the community or in school. However, the coach can 'make haste slowly': they might become aware that this is an issue they will have to report, but they can take some time to use the group to facilitate a discussion about what others think could or should be done to help their fellow participant. The group, again, can be seen as a resource, as Sue Young has described in her invaluable book on ways of using the SF approach in working with individuals and groups in schools where bullying has been identified (Young 2009).

The location for the groupwork is an important issue to decide in advance. In the case of the anger-management group, the room allocation changed each week – a not untypical event in a school. This led to an unfortunate circumstance. All the sessions took place in empty classrooms. On one occasion, as the meeting was in progress, the teacher to whom the classroom belonged came into the room. There are no prizes for guessing the precise moment he chose to enter. Yes, it was the 'tuck break'. And there are no prizes for guessing that this particular teacher was regarded as tough and old fashioned, someone who had no sympathy with what he regarded as 'do-gooder' types. So he looked at what was going on in his room, got some books out, and proceeded to sit down and demonstrate what real work looked like. It took a great measure of self will on my part to quietly approach him and explain that, odd as it looked, this was actually serious groupwork – and that, now the boys had finished their 2-minute breather, they were going to carry on working and, 'umm, would you mind. . .?'. Thankfully, he obliged and left the room. I said a quick prayer of thanks and got back to work.

References

Campbell, T.C. and Brasher, B. (1994) The pause that refreshes: opportunities, interventions and predictions in group therapy with cocaine addicts. *Journal of Systemic Therapies* 13(2): 65–73.

Emanuel, C. (2005) Solution Focused Groups in Primary Schools. Handout for Solutions in Education Conference organised by BRIEF 13 May.

Iveson, C. (2014) Personal communication.

Kelly, M., Kim, J. and Franklin, C. (2008) *Solution Focused Brief Therapy in Schools: a 360-degree View of Research & Practice*. Oxford: Oxford University Press.

Metcalf, L. (1998) *Solution Focused Group Therapy*. New York: Simon & Schuster.

O'Hanlon, B. (1995) Problems and Possibilities. Presentation to BRIEF, 9–10 November, London.

O'Hanlon, B. and Beadle, S. (1994) *A Field Guide to PossibilityLand*. London: BT Press.

Pichot, T. with Smock, S.A. (2009) *Solution-Focused Substance Abuse Treatment*. Abingdon: Routledge.

Sharry, J. (2007) *Solution Focused Groupwork*, 2nd ed. London: Sage.

Wade, A. (1997) Small acts of living: everyday resistance to violence and other forms of oppression. *Contemporary Family Therapy* 19: 23–39.

Young, S. (2009) *Solution-Focused Schools: Anti-Bullying and Beyond*. London: BT Press.

Chapter 6

In the school

Why coach in a school?

A Solution Focused Brief Coaching (SFBC) service for children and young people is a cost-effective way to promote wellbeing, achievement and collaborative behaviour. Its strength base and future focus fits with an educational philosophy aimed at bringing out the best of each student. Because of this fit, the approach has proved effective well beyond the individual coaching session and is easily applicable across the whole of the school community. For example, as others have shown (Rhodes and Ajmal 1995; Ajmal and Rees 2001; Metcalf 2008; Kelly et al 2008; Young 2009; Ratner et al 2012), the model can be used in working with reading difficulties, groups, in classroom management, in corridors, in playground organisation, in parent meetings, in staff meetings, in consultations, and in many other ways throughout the education system.

Many schools now have coaches coming into the school, and although this is a significant cost, when it is effective it pays for itself in many ways. With a maximum of half-hour sessions, an SF coach can see quite a number of students in a morning – and in the process, because in schools a little goes a long way, transform the lives of students and staff alike. However, not all schools can afford the luxury of a coach, and they may have more children in need than their coach can handle.

In these circumstances, students in need must rely on the school's pastoral staff, many of whom will have a disciplinary role in addition to that of care-giver. SFBC lends itself very well to this role. It can be hard for a student to reveal problems and vulnerabilities to a person he or she must deal with in other contexts, and it can be equally hard for teachers to take on a student's vulnerability when the student is also disrupting classes. SFBC, with its strength base and future focus, promotes aspirational conversations. This does not mean that teachers are absolved from hearing of a student's difficulties (and sometimes taking action in relation to them) but it does allow a safe way forward without delving unnecessarily deeply into the student's life. Students themselves are quick to recognise that this form of coaching is not going to be 'painful' in any way, and for the most part they report enjoying the sessions.

The fact that SFBC does not probe into problems is so counter-intuitive that students will raise as many questions as professionals. 'Surely you need to know what the problem is before you can solve it!' is usually the first response of students learning the approach for a peer counselling service (Hillel & Smith 2001). And this would be true if people were like car engines – a single machine with no possibilities other than those it was built for. However, as every teacher and parent knows, children have untold potential and creative capacity. SFBC relies on this potential and, like teaching itself, aims to build on this rather than understand its absence. This does not mean that the search to understand problems is invalid, but from a pragmatic point of view it is more productive to resolve problems as quickly as possible and reserve more time for consuming and costly investigations in those situations where SFBC has not worked.

The SF coach is therefore not trained in analysing and understanding what is wrong but rather in 'conversational skills' which help a student put things right. The SF coach is also trained to draw out each student's often hidden resources and place them at his or her disposal for the task of finding a new way forward. The skill of the coach is not to know what the student should do but to bring the student to that knowledge himself or herself. This reliance on the student's personal knowledge also helps the coach avoid bumping into, or even trampling on, the cultural sensitivities of students. It is the student who tells the coach how her world works rather than the coach telling the student how it should be run. Not that the coach, especially if she is also a teacher, is entirely without a say. A school may require students to dress or behave in a way that may not always fit completely with their cultural norms; this, like codes of behaviour and an expectation of learning, is part of the wider contract between school, students, parents and society and is usually not up for negotiation.

In summary, an SFBC service has a number of advantages:

- It can accommodate a high number of referrals.
- It can complete the work quickly.
- It creates a positive frame of mind for students.
- Students miss less school work.
- Students are more able to take charge of themselves and improve in self efficacy skills.
- It provides a structure for a different strand of conversation with children outside the normal teacher–student dialogue.
- As children are more in touch with their successes than their difficulties, their confidence grows and they are often able to sort the difficulties out for themselves.
- Because it focuses so much on positive interactions, peer relationships within the classroom often improve.

Feedback from teachers and parents on SFBC programmes often pick up on these points:

- *Children were able to reflect on their strengths and areas for development and given time to talk about progress. Having one to one time is very rare and this was an excellent resource to help children meet challenges.* (HT Primary School)

- *The children all grew in confidence and independence, and it was helpful for them to be able to reflect on themselves and their learning in this way.* (Teacher Year 5 Class)

- *It really helped her to develop a sense of herself and her own ability to change things.* (Parent)

- *She has become less anxious and developed more positive relationships with her peers.* (Parent)

Coaching and pastoral care

Most schools are proud of the pastoral care they offer their students but are often challenged by the need to preserve discipline. The unique needs of one child cannot always be met if the cost to the rest of the school, through disruption for instance, is too high. And when a student with obvious abilities is heading towards exclusion, a Year Head is likely to feel torn apart by the competing need to care for the student and care for the school. Once again, SFBC offers no panacea but it does provide a framework, consistent with most school philosophies, and relatively simple to adopt, which increases the likelihood of such seemingly intractable conflicts reaching a more than satisfactory resolution.

The good fit between a school's vision for every child to do the best they can, and SFBC's interest in children recognising the strengths and skills which will enable them to build successful futures, provides the foundation for the successful introduction of an SF approach to pastoral care. Perhaps the most useful outcome of this fit is that SF conversations do not need to be confined to the 'hallowed' walls of a counselling room; once they have begun they can take place in snatches – in the corridors, for a minute or so at the start or finish of classes, and at the school gates as students arrive. What makes this possible when, with many other coaching models, it would be quite inappropriate, is that SF conversations are founded on the student's own hopes for the future and the past successes on which this future could be built. If a student is seen misbehaving in a corridor a teacher might tell him or her off, and issue a warning, or might take the opportunity to remind the student of their ambitions and past success with a question which tacitly notes the bad behaviour while offering an alternative: 'If this turned into another of those "good days" you had last week, what might your next teacher notice as you walk into the classroom?'. Or a student who has had a day of misbehaving but without going so far as being excluded might be asked: 'What did you do to stop yourself getting excluded?'. And, 'If tomorrow turns out to be a better day for you what will your friends notice about you when you arrive in the morning?'. These questions, which chart past successes and trace out possible futures, are the nuts and bolts of SF conversations, and almost every question that might be asked in a formal coaching session can also be asked as part of the everyday conversations between staff and students in schools.

Many staff are also interested in having formal SFBC sessions with their pupils too. One of the difficulties for them in doing this is that their own role is sometimes a determining factor in what the student has to work on, and leads to an investment in a particular outcome, which can make it difficult to coach effectively. It can also at times be difficult for a teacher who knows a student well to consistently ask questions with a genuine sense of curiosity rather than questions which have a right answer lurking in their shadows. However, some staff find that they can deal with these issues by being clear with the student (and themselves) that the coaching role they are taking, in that particular session, is a bit different from their other role or roles.

The 'external' coach

If you have been hired by the school it is important to be clear about the reasons for the school's decision to employ a coach, their view of the task, and their criteria for success. Early discussions about this almost always prevent later misunderstandings. If it is possible to spend some time in staff rooms it will be easier for the staff to understand and support the coach and easier for the coach to fit into the school. I have found it useful to use the SFBC model in all the formal and informal conversations I have had in a school, whether they are informal conversations in the staff room or corridor, or more formal consultations or meetings. For example, a teacher and I were chatting for a few minutes at the coffee machine in the staff room before school started:

Teacher: Oh, I'm not at my best today! I'm dreading my next class.
Coach: So what would the class notice about you as you came through the door if you were at your best?
Teacher: Hmm (*thoughtful pause*). I'll let you know later!

Steve de Shazer said that SF conversations were 'nothing but a bunch of talk' (de Shazer 1994: 3), and in my experience *doing* the talk rather than *explaining* the talk is a more effective way to increase everyone's understanding.

Schools have their own policies, protocols and procedures, and it helps if the SF coach is aware of them, not least for the student's sake. One student at a second session said nothing was better, and stuck by this for the whole 20-minute session. It was only later, in the staff room, that his form tutor remarked on genuine attempts by the boy to cooperate with the school's dress code. The boy had stopped wearing trainers to school. If the coach had been aware of the significance of the shoes an entirely different second session might have evolved.

Client–coach contract

A coach's primary purpose is to provide a 'client service', to work with the client towards an end the client hopes to achieve. Nonetheless, what a coach will work towards is not entirely at the discretion of the client. In the worlds of business or sport it would be unthinkable to accept a contract to increase absence from work or give up tennis (if that were the sport). Similarly, within a school, a coach can only work towards outcomes that fit within the wider contract between student and school. For example, it would not be appropriate to work towards a student truanting. Harry Korman describes useful criteria for the SF practitioner in agreeing a contract with their client, suggesting that it should be something that the client wishes to achieve, which fits in with the practitioner's legitimate remit, and which the client and practitioner could hope to achieve together (Korman 2004). When students do come up with a hope that is unrealistic, for example never having to come to school again, the coach can be sure that the student is perfectly aware of the situation and not serious about the unrealistic outcome.

Coach: What are your best hopes from this meeting?
Student: I'll be allowed to choose the lessons I want to go to.
Coach: What are the chances of that happening?
Student: Zero.
Coach: Okay, so you are a realist. What else do you hope for?
Student: Attitude – I need to have a better attitude.

It is also essential for coaches (and all professionals involved with the school) to be fully aware of the school's child-protection policy and the limits it places on confidentiality. This should be made clear to each student at the very start of coaching and the coach needs to remember that safety, of the student or anyone else, always takes precedence over confidentiality. Coaches need to know what to do in a school when they find themselves working with young people who show risky behaviours – such as self-harm, drug taking, offending, or sexual behaviour – or who are, or have been, affected by issues of child abuse. SFBC is not a risk-assessment model, and the coach will need to move 'out of model' to make a risk assessment and consider making a referral to the school child-protection officer. If the young person has other agencies working with them to assess, manage and reduce the risks to them, the coach may find themselves working alongside these other professionals in offering a school-based coaching service.

In practice, SFBC raises fewer confidentiality issues than coaching models that investigate problems. Though permission to pass on information must always be obtained, most students are happy for the coach to share their successes and ambitions with key members of staff. When a school, as a whole, adopts an SF approach, the work of individual coaching sessions can be expanded throughout the whole school day. The form tutor who commented favourably on the student's footwear probably achieved in 20 seconds more than the coach did in 20 minutes.

It is helpful to agree the formal and informal sharing of information at the point a service is established. Some schools ask that the students' 'best hopes' and summaries of progress be made available to staff so that they could target their support more accurately. As long as students are aware of such protocols they should raise no problems.

Information also needs to travel the other way. The coach needs to be informed of outcomes so that the service can prove its worth. The more closely coaching outcomes are aligned to existing school measures the easier and more convincing will be the argument that coaching works. Most schools have systems of behaviour (good and bad) monitoring, and as many referrals for coaching are behaviour-related, effective coaching should make a difference to the student's report card.

Agreeing the best hopes

It is not always easy to discover the best hopes of the child or young person from coaching but in most cases it is surprisingly straightforward. Misbehaving primary-school children are rarely happy and mostly would like to be happier. Unhappy primary-school children behave in ways which worry their teachers and parents. When they are helped to describe their own ways of being happy they will often do so in terms of their relationships – with family, friends and teachers. Happy children tend to behave well because the positive feedback they receive encourages more. Similarly, as children experience improvements in their behaviour they experience the positive feedback and become happier. In secondary schools the motivation is more commonly to get good exam results. Few teenagers will be unaware of the massive disadvantage to future employment a poor school record creates, and though they might not yet have found a way to 'do' school well they have usually not given up trying. But whether straightforward or not, an SF coaching session cannot proceed without an agreed contract between student and coach: the question 'What are your best hopes from this coaching?' needs to have a mutually agreeable answer. Because this answer defines the purpose and hoped-for end of the work it must capture the imagination and motivation of the student rather than the rules and regulations of the school. Traditional behavioural targets such as 'I will not be abusive verbally or physically to students or staff' is a legitimate requirement of the school but not one that will fire up a student to strive in a new direction. The student above is likely to be referred for 'anger management', a policy which requires the problem (anger) to continue to exist for it to work.

Coach: What are your best hopes from meeting with me?
Student: Anger. Anger management.
Coach: What difference do you hope managing your anger will make?
Student: I won't be in so much trouble and I'll get on with my work better.
Coach: And what difference do you hope that will make?
Student: I'll have more chance of getting a better job – and be happier, I suppose.
Coach: So if this meeting helps you get on with your work more and in a way
   that makes you feel happier will that mean that it has been useful?
Student: Definitely.

In this way the student is led towards a more obviously beneficial outcome that, by implication, fits the behavioural standards of the school. Once again, it is important to remember that, however difficult it may be, coach and client need to establish an outcome for the work because until we know that we will not be able to ask the questions that we need to ask.

In secondary schools it is often not possible to meet with the member of staff most concerned about a child. They are just too busy getting on with a packed timetable of their own. However, when it is possible to meet beforehand it can be very useful to ask for their best hopes with respect to the student. This does not mean that the professional's hopes will supersede those of the student but hopefully the coach will be able to keep both in mind while shaping the conversation. Not surprisingly, student and staff hoped-for outcomes are rarely out of synch. It is almost impossible to do well in school without maintaining the bulk of the school's rules. Less conflict leads to less stress, greater wellbeing and general happiness. This is so obvious it sounds trite yet it is not uncommon for professionals to express surprise at student–staff accord. The following examples show how closely aligned student and staff hoped-for outcomes usually are.

Examples of the best hopes of referrers from a school coaching service

- For him to feel better about himself and more confident about coming to school

- For him to act more appropriately in school and in lessons

- To make better relationships with peers

- To improve her confidence and manage her feelings

- To develop more focus and more coping strategies

Examples of the best hopes of secondary-school students from a school coaching service

- To be able to ignore bad comments, be able to go out and not be scared

- To increase my confidence, especially around other students

- To be able to handle difficult situations

- To feel more happy and relaxed at school

- To improve my work and my friendships

- To be able to get more work done, be organised, and ignore trouble

- To control my anger and keep calmer in lessons

But there is not always total accord. Students who do not toe the line might also be strong-willed and keen to show their independence alongside their co-operation. The boy who wore shoes put them on at the school gate, returning to his trainers at lunch time and at the end of the day. A girl who returned to school after a long period of frequent truanting decided that she would attend 80.5% of the term, 0.5% above the cut-off point for statutory action against her and her family. She was pursuing her own ambition to get a place at art school while maintaining, at least in spirit, her opposition to what she thought was an oppressive educational regime. Such quid pro quos are common where there is a statutory component to the work. A young person might agree to conform with one set of demands simply to achieve a higher purpose. In schools, therefore, coaches will at times have to adopt a 'twin track' approach, operating a 'client track' and an 'agency track' at the same time (Ratner et al 2012: 89–90). This is a useful approach when the school is concerned that a particular issue be addressed, but the child or young person is unconcerned. It is often possible to find something the young person *does* want to work on, and then invite them to work on both issues.

Examples of the best hopes of primary-school children from coaching

- Stop worrying about everything and feel more relaxed
- Be better at sports
- Get faster at times tables
- Use better words in my writing
- Be braver
- Stick up for myself more
- Keep focused
- Help more at home
- Get on better with my mum
- Be more generous
- Make more friends
- Speak more in class
- Be able to say no more to people
- Listen more
- Manage when I'm angry so I can stay in class
- Stay calm with my friends
- Tell the truth more and not lie to people

Finally, when establishing a contract, we, as adults, have to guard against knowing what is best for the student. The fact that we probably do know best is irrelevant because that knowledge, which comes from experience, cannot be passed on. Instead, our job is to help the child come to his or her own answers and we do this by asking questions with a genuine sense of curiosity and with a mind free of possible answers. Establishing the child's or young person's best hopes from the work in this way may take time in the beginning, but it prevents many wasted journeys later.

Resource talk

After exploring answers to the 'best hopes' question, and before moving on to questions about the young person's preferred future, it is possible to introduce 'resource talk'. This is a problem-free way of getting to know the client, and can be particularly useful when a student is not appearing to engage very well. It can become a route to what the student wants to achieve.

Jed, 14

An example is of a Year 9 student, Jed, who came to a session and said that he had no idea why he was there or what his best hopes from the coaching might be. He also didn't know what anyone else's best hopes for him from the coaching might be, and I had no prior information myself (not unusual in a busy secondary school trying to keep paperwork to a minimum). He kept whistling and looking up at the ceiling. Eventually, I asked him what he was good at. He said football, and in response to my question 'What made a good footballer?' he became much more responsive, highlighting 'good communication' and 'setting an example' as two important skills. We were then able to move on to discussing which subjects he was good at in school and art was top of his list. However, Jed still did not appear very engaged in the session so I looked further into the future and asked about his career hopes. Surprisingly, he wanted to be an engineer but was so disaffected with his science teacher that he walked out of most lessons. When I asked him if he would prefer to stay in his lessons he gave me a slightly pityingly look: 'Of course'. Almost every session, even the most challenging, will provide an entry point to a creative conversation, and this was it. 'Let's imagine that, when you come into school tomorrow, science has been transformed and has become a class in which you can work hard and succeed. What is the first thing you will notice as you walk into the room?' This question, treated at first with disdain, soon led to a long and detailed description of a great science lesson which naturally included the communication and example-setting skills that Jed had identified as so important in football. This took up most of the session but still left me time to ask him about the times he had managed to stay in the lesson and what he had learned about himself from that. Then off he went whistling, just as he did when he arrived. I learned afterwards that Jed had been on the point of exclusion but had managed to improve his behaviour to avoid this.

There are advantages and disadvantages to having prior information about students. In some ways it is easier to know nothing. In the example above, if I had known that the boy was so close to exclusion I might have challenged him when he claimed that he had no idea why he was there. And with the challenge I would probably have lost him. As it was I had no choice but to work exclusively within his frame and trust both him and the coaching process. In this case the trust paid off. Coaches will differ in the amount of information they want to know about a student, but for those who are prepared to rely more exclusively on what the student brings, a good rule of thumb is to ask the referrer to give you whatever information they think is absolutely necessary for you to know beforehand. This is another way to fit with the school and with variations within the school. One referrer might want to tell you the student's life story while another might decide that you need to know only very basic information.

Staying impartial

There is much that, at first sight, is counter-intuitive in SFBC, and one unlikely finding from practice is that the more we try to promote changes the slower those changes will happen, if they happen at all. As a result, we have taught ourselves the important discipline of impartiality in relation to outcome. This does not mean that we are insensitive and unconcerned about a student's happiness or distress nor does it mean that we don't care what happens to them tomorrow. It is just that the more we take it upon ourselves to generate change, to find solutions, the less invested the student becomes. This impartiality is sometimes difficult to maintain in a school setting where professionals are working with clear ideas about good outcomes for children, and views about how those outcomes should be achieved. SF coaches, too, want their clients to achieve their hopes and ambitions. At present it is a case of learning from practice: our outcomes are better when we do not push for change and instead concentrate on drawing out descriptions of what change might look like. For instance, rather than asking what a student 'needs to do' to effect a small change we will ask 'what difference will the student notice' *if* such a small change were made. Why this should be more effective is not clear to us, although it may have something to do with the coach not working harder than the student and trying to push the student in a particular direction. Once the coach begins to want the outcome more, the student may want it less, and we may begin to construct resistance which was not there before. We may also stop listening for the student's own best way forward, and miss small details, resources or directions which would be an important part of a successful outcome.

Staying on the surface

'Too often people who want to learn SFBT fall into the trap of not being able to see that the difficulty is to stay on the surface when the temptation to look behind and beneath is at its strongest' (de Shazer, quoted in Lee et al 2003: 18).

For many years the dominant discourse of psychological, developmental or performance-enhancing help was problem-centred, and conversations about problems in schools were seen as the best way to help children. This was not without good reason. At face value it is logical to think that problems need to be understood, that we need to get to the bottom of them, in order for solutions to be found: it is the scientific, medical model which is now deeply embedded in western culture. Schools are also *in loco parentis* and need to care for their charges in a more parental way – listening to each child's everyday struggles, big or small, and doing their best to help them to feel secure enough to fulfil their educational potential. Coaching provides one way of fulfilling this responsibility when the more routine pastoral provision is not enough.

It is at this point that a different sort of conversation takes place; traditionally, it has been a conversation which probes the problem, seeking to identify the cause and rectify the damage. This approach is certainly not without its successes but it can be painful, can also take a long time (sometimes too long when a student is on the edge of exclusion) and, unfortunately, can carry the weight of stigma which, in some cases, is too high a price for the child to pay.

It is not surprising, therefore, that school professionals are increasingly turning towards the SF approach as a way of reaching more children and doing so with less risk to their peer status within the school. Some schools have found the approach so beneficial that they have adapted it to every level of their operation and called themselves 'solution focused schools', such as the Garza Independence High School in Austin, Texas (Kelly et al 2008; http://garzaindependencehs. weebly.com) and FKC in Stockholm (Mahlberg & Sjoblom 2004). However, the SF approach can still seem unusual to some school professionals, particularly in the lack of attention the coach will pay to the problem.

SF coaches are not problem phobic, and in schools it is vital that all staff, including coaches, are as aware as they can be of what their students are struggling with – this is part of providing a safe and caring environment. They will listen to problems but they are unlikely to ask for problem details or think about problem causation because they have a different approach to the conversation. Instead, they will want to help the student build a detailed and realistic description of life without the problem, a description of an alternative yet possible future and a description of their past achievements which might form a foundation for this future. These descriptions of past and possible experiences are taken absolutely at face value, there is no attempt to interpret what they might mean, no going beneath the surface looking for hidden meanings or explanations. The information is not used to build an 'understanding' of the child according to a psychological theory so that we can then 'fix' the child, it is actually for the child to hear and learn from his or her own words. The coach does not ask questions to learn about the child, she asks questions so that students can learn about themselves – their strengths, resources and possibilities.

Being able to stay on the surface and not dig for more problem details and possible explanations is one of the core skills of an SF coach, one that is both challenging to learn and fundamental to the success of the work. However, to other professionals not familiar with SFBC it might seem to be adopting a superficial approach which does not address real problems. The SF coach may find themselves being offered more and more problem-based information or may find that their service is pigeon-holed as a 'soft' approach dealing with superficial or non-serious issues, although SFBC works effectively with a wide range of issues and problems. In these circumstances I have found that it can sometimes be useful to explain some of the thinking and techniques behind the approach to colleagues. At other times I have found that this can be experienced as proselytising, and that it is more respectful to explain less and do more.

Maryam, 12

Maryam, a Year 7 child, was referred by John, a very experienced education support worker with the school support unit. Maryam did not like to speak in lessons or tutorials, or with any of the school staff. She spoke only with her friends in school and with her family at home. The school was concerned about her learning and development although she was making reasonable progress in her work. Maryam had spoken in her primary school classes although she had been described as very quiet. John's best hope from the coaching was for Maryam to be able to speak in school lessons, and with the staff, and be able to participate in school life more fully.

I started work with Maryam using pens and paper and she drew or wrote things and nodded and shook her head in the first session, and spoke only a little. In the second session she spoke more easily with me although she still continued to draw and write and enjoyed this. She was now able to tell me that she, too, wanted to be able to speak in lessons because she wanted to become a doctor – an ambition which, until then, she had shared with no one. We framed her best hope from coaching as doing all the things she could do now which would help her towards her dream of being a doctor.

SF questions help children and young people to explore and get to know *themselves*, not as a 'child-with-problems' but as a resourceful person with ambitions and possibilities. Maryam began making drawings of which lessons she might speak in first, and on the table in her picture of where she would be sitting she wrote the words she hoped to say. She drew her friends smiling at her and other students looking surprised. Some teachers had big smiles on their faces, because they secretly knew she would do this, while others, such as some of the students, were surprised. Maryam also wanted to do more homework and reading to help her work improve. She drew herself doing homework on the kitchen table when she got in from school, and reading in bed. Talking more loudly at home was also one of her ambitions so she drew herself speaking louder than her sisters and with a louder voice when her dad got in from work, so he could hear something important about her day. In these conversations the coach is always listening for signs of the future already happening by questions such as 'Would your dad be surprised by your louder voice or does it sometimes happen?'. During her descriptions, Maryam began to realise many things she was already doing but had not noticed because she was focusing on her silence. She had already spoken once or twice in small group activities during lessons, and, with pride, she remembered that she had taken part in a group presentation to her class by introducing the presentation with a sentence. She had forgotten that she had done this, and, so it seemed, had many others! She also noticed that she was reading in bed sometimes and doing more of her homework, and had managed to get her dad to hear her first when he got in because she needed to ask for some money for a school trip.

After the first few sessions the school noticed a little bit of improvement: Maryam was talking very quietly with one of the teaching assistants in one of her classes. During one of my regular discussions with John he asked if I had found out why Maryam hadn't been talking in school. I said I hadn't. 'Why do you think she hasn't been talking then?' he persisted. 'I don't know', I said. After more questions from John about possible reasons, and disappointing responses from me, I asked John about Maryam's progress. John said he was pleased with her progress.

In subsequent sessions Maryam began to build up a story of herself in which talking more in school was meaningful to her in her own special way. Exploring what she did, how she did it, and what qualities she saw in herself helped her to consolidate and celebrate this story.

Questions of identity

Questions of identity can be especially useful when working in schools, where in spite of schools' efforts to promote positive, appreciative cultures there is often a need for students to combat negative stories about themselves perpetrated by others; for example, 'she's a bully', 'he's no good at sports', 'he's a loner', 'she starts rumours'. Older children and teenagers are particularly prone to anxieties about who they are, what they can do and how they are seen, and negative stories or stories of deficit can take hold quickly. Using questions about identity, from the child's own and their significant others' perspectives, can be very powerful in addressing these anxieties during the course of coaching. For example, when we hear of any success, recent or in the more distant past, we can ask: 'What does this tell you about yourself?'. Or we can tie future success to past experience with questions like: 'Which of your friends knows you well enough to believe that you can achieve these hopes?'. 'Strength cards' (Chapter 8) are very helpful in building a positive identity. Sorting through the pack for cards that identify aspects of the student's recent positive behaviour at the start of a session, or during a session, can help them to identify what qualities they drew on in a particular instance. If it is also in line with their best hopes, they might choose one quality that they are going to notice a bit more in their actions in the next week. Sometimes they might ask a friend to look out for when they see this too. And if the coach is part of the school staff he or she might also look out for evidence of the identified skills and qualities.

Not the miracle worker!

It can happen that what might seem to the coach to have been a useful coaching session is immediately followed by inappropriate behaviour outside the session. Whilst the client is the prime expert on whether a coaching session has been useful, any stakeholders in the process will also have a view. Coaching in a school is highly visible to stakeholders, and the coach can feel under pressure to perform miracles. However, these 'episodes' outside the coaching room can be helpful because they remind us of the modest role we play in many of the miracles which children and young people perform themselves.

The reality of the work is that children and young people may be taking small steps and making small changes, and these will not always be immediately visible to the school. There can also be setbacks, and these can be an opportunity for the coach to help the young person to explore how they have managed to keep going, or what skill and strength they have drawn on to face the setback and try new things. If the setback was obviously visible to you (outside your door, for example), you may choose to refer to it in the next session, or the young person themselves might tell you about it. Questions such as 'How come it wasn't worse?', 'When were the times this week you were able to turn things around?' or 'What did you notice about how you dealt with this setback which was better?' are opportunities for the young person to continue to notice what has been different and more in line with what they want to see happening. Dealing with setbacks is a skill which it is useful for children and young people to develop, and if you ask them how they have managed setbacks in the past you will help them to uncover many coping mechanisms and strategies they may not have noticed themselves using.

Ali, 12

I worked with a Year 7 boy, Ali, at his request, as well as at the school's request, on managing his anger. This was causing him a lot of problems. He wanted to be able to keep himself calm instead of getting angry, and in the first session he wrote a list of what keeping calm would look like for him and what difference it would make to his life. In the second session he was very pleased to talk about what he had noticed in the last week which had been better, and we explored these things in detail. As soon as he left the session, he joined one of his classes and became embroiled in a verbal and physical fight with another boy; he even picked up a chair. In the third session Ali told me what had happened. He expressed remorse and I asked him what was keeping him motivated to keep trying and he said that he wanted to make his mum proud of him. We talked about how he had managed similar difficulties in the past. It seemed that his mum was often proud of him for resisting temptation and for getting himself back under control when he was very angry. He also noticed that although he had picked up the chair, on that occasion he had not thrown it anywhere, nor even got as far as aiming it through the classroom window. On previous occasions he had taken aim, although someone in the class had always prevented the aim turning into a throw. Instead, this time he had stopped himself and had put the chair down. He thought that, although he had been subject to an internal exclusion for the fight, there might be some seeds of pride for his mum too. This made him happier, and the setback became a step in the right direction for him too. He just hadn't noticed.

Ali's 'keeping calm' list: what it will look like for him

1   Speaking nicely to the neighbour at 7 a.m. if the neighbour is playing music loudly (not shouting)

2   Saying 'Good morning' to his family (not arguing)

3   Saying 'Goodbye' to his family

4   No shouting in the house before he leaves even if he is late

5   Asking people 'Are you OK?' in football games

6   Accepting it if people tackle him, especially slide tackles

7   Walking away if someone cusses him in the playground

8   Tutor Mrs R would see him smiling

9   Saying 'yes' or 'sorry' in class and not arguing back

10   Even if something seems unfair no shouting at the teacher

11   Being less moody and more fun so friends aren't scared of him and ask him to play more

12   Being relaxed and maybe going to more clubs because he is not afraid of getting into trouble

13   Asking to go to the Support Unit, which is a good place to calm down

14   Remembering that some things don't matter that much to him

---

Giving homework

Sometimes I have asked students if it is OK to give them homework. They often look at me aghast, until I suggest that they watch out for what they do which is in line with what they want to have happen. They often enjoy the idea that this is homework. Other homework I might suggest is 'try something new and tell me about it next time', or I might ask them to act as if their hoped-for future has already begun and see what happens. The idea of acting without committing themselves often appeals to young people, and the act could then be explored in more detail in the next session. With some young people I have found that giving them a homework task helps them to remember and focus on what they want, particularly if they have a lot going on in their lives. On the other hand, homework is often not done so it is important when giving homework not to *need* it done for the next session – if it's not done it shouldn't matter.

Involving teachers, learning mentors and pastoral support workers

The people who make the referrals to the coach in the school are involved in the coaching work to the extent that they have a good reason for making the referral and therefore some best hopes for its outcome. However, they may be a link in the referral system, reporting someone else's best hopes from the coaching for the child. Sometimes referrers may be teachers or heads of year, but more often in large or busy schools it will be the pastoral support workers or learning support unit staff who will be the link and main referral source. These staff may be referring young people known to them in their own unit or other pupils for whom teaching staff have requested the service.

Sometimes the referrer or pastoral link worker can be invited into the first session, or part of the session or subsequent sessions. Sometimes it is the student who requests this, or it may be that the referrer asks to come in and share their 'best hopes'. Learning mentors who come as an ally to support a student can be a wonderful resource in coaching sessions, encouraging the student to answer, reminding the student of examples of resources or progress they have seen in the week, or generally amplifying anything which has been done well. Their relationship with the student as a mentor allows them to express their own views in this way, which is different to the coach's role but can be vitalising in a session.

Working with translators in sessions can seem challenging at times. However, it can also be an opportunity to slow things down – for extra thinking time on all sides, and for taking the 'attention pressure' off the young person; in my experience, it can be a lot of fun too. Translators can be surprised at the questions, and this can lead to more energy in the room, or they may know and like the SF approach and offer a lot of encouragement to the student. It was due to one translator's total confidence in the student in a session that the student was able to complete a list of 25 things they had been pleased to notice about themselves in the last week.

Sometimes pastoral support workers or mentors attend sessions intermittently. This gives a good opportunity for the student to rehearse before them what has gone particularly well since they were previously there. Using the 'other person's perspective' whilst the person is actually in the room seems to multiply possibilities: you can ask the student what they think the learning mentor has noticed before you ask the learning mentor, and vice versa. Students can also ask their mentor to carry on looking out for certain things in their behaviour and compliment them in between sessions on this behaviour. This can increase motivation in the student and a sense of consolidating progress. Using scales can be a way of student and mentor talking in code rather than openly in public, which can be important to some students.

Some students have enjoyed inviting a learning mentor or pastoral worker to their final session to celebrate all the changes they have made. This is possible only if the coach and the student can plan the final session, rather than identify it in retrospect. In one school I worked in, the coaching project involved students having up to six coaching sessions and it was often possible for students to invite a staff member to their final session. This would involve juice, cakes and compliments, not only to the student, but from the student to the staff member for their help.

Sharing information protocols can be discussed and set up in advance, but often information which is shared may need more discussion, because it can mean different things to different professionals, as in the following example.

Felipe, 14

Felipe wanted to stand up for himself more and talk more. He liked his tutor, who was giving him a lot of support, and he was happy for his tutor to be given informal feedback on his progress. I was sitting in the staff room one day and mentioned to his tutor that Felipe was pleased with himself this week and had put himself at 8 on his scale. She looked very surprised. 'I don't think he is at an 8 yet' she said, 'definitely not, maybe a 6 or a 5'. We talked about the scale's importance in demonstrating movement, rather than any fixed values, but more importantly, we talked about what Felipe might have noticed about himself this week which told him he was at an 8 *on his scale*. We also talked about what she might notice about him when he moved up from the 6 to the 7 or 8 *on her scale*. We talked about her confidence in his progress, and why it was so high, and where his classmates in her view might have put him on a scale this week. She wondered *where he would think she would put him* on his scale and asked me to ask him in the next session. The scale moved from being an overall judgement tool to a tool unlocking many possibilities for change.

Classroom coaching – WOWW!

WOWW is the brainchild of Insoo Kim Berg and Lee Shilts (Berg & Shilts 2005; Shilts 2013) and stands for Working on What Works. It might be better stated as 'watching out for what works' because the essence of the classroom model is one of observation. On the principle that what is working well is often overlooked, especially when specific students have been labelled as 'difficult', then, as the teacher can't have eyes at the back and sides of her head, an observer will be an invaluable asset in spotting children doing well.

To ensure that teachers do not see the exercise as another means of monitoring their teaching abilities, it is important that those classes identified for the 'project' have the voluntary cooperation of the teachers concerned. The teachers will have an introductory meeting with the coach to discuss the way the project will be run, and what they hope everyone will gain from it.

The structure of the model is simple. After the introductory staff meeting, the coach is introduced to the class at the start of a lesson. We have found that it is of benefit for a senior manager to be present at this initial introduction to help emphasise its importance and value to everyone. The class is told that the coach will simply be observing how the lesson goes, and when there is 5 minutes left she will tell the class all the good things she has observed. This model of observation is repeated a number of times with different lessons with that particular class or year group. How many times the observations are done will depend on many factors. One teacher told us (Ratner et al 2012) that it should be ten times but we have managed to run the project on as few as four per lesson, spread out over several weeks. At the half-way stage, the staff meet to discuss progress with the coach and to iron out any difficulties. At the end of the project there is a further meeting to review things.

We have found that the staff meetings are very valuable. Time for meetings is at a premium in schools, which is why the involvement of a senior manager to support the project is crucial. The coach runs the meetings in SF style: asking questions about what progress has already been noted, what will be signs of further progress, and using scales to explore differing perceptions of the progress.

The actual process of classroom observation involves the coach in making swift and detailed notes on everything and anything he sees that seems to go well. Gestures of cooperation with the teacher and with other students, quiet working periods, good questions asked and answered, the way disputes or bad behaviour are ended (rather than why they started!) and so on. We have found that it is beneficial for us to walk around the classroom from time to time, and to ask students for their names. It has been common at the end to find oneself with a list of nearly 30 items of what worked well and so the coach only needs to read out a few of them and to name the students concerned (always a boon to those highlighted!). It is possible to vary the approach as the observations continue. For example, we have found it useful to engage the students playfully in guessing how many things are on the coach's list. This has been particularly valuable when the lesson went badly, as the students expect few or no observations to have been made and are delighted when the coach reveals the (few!) things they came up with. Scales can also be introduced, and another technique is to ask a class at the start of a lesson what is their expectation of how well today's lesson will go, so that this can be reviewed at the end of the lesson.

Notice that it is entirely about the students. The coach usually makes no reference to what the teacher did, although they could compliment something they were particularly impressed by. Most teachers value a few minutes with the coach after the lesson to discuss things. This is another reason why the staff meetings are so valuable. In Berg/Shilts' model (op. cit.) there is information about how the classroom coach can also use the SF model to coach individual teachers.

Feedback we have received from the projects we have run has indicated that students have benefited considerably in terms of behavioural change and how the class has gelled as a community. As one Year 8 student said:

'Telling us what we done good that's like an achievement, saying you've achieved a lot, and people want to keep it up so that they can get more compliments, and the more compliments they get the better phone calls home they get . . . their parents are happy, they're happy, so it's actually made it a lot better, in school and out'

(Ratner et al op. cit.: 191)

Staff coaching in schools

Some SF coaches are able to offer teachers, and other education staff, coaching sessions in the school for professional or personal issues alongside a coaching service for the students. The straightforward nature of the approach, its brevity, and its future focus makes it attractive to staff and their managers, and the focus on the person's own resources and ideas for how things could be better or happier for them means that the coach does not have to have any special expertise or knowledge of education issues; in fact, such expertise would be likely to get in the way of coaching effectively. In the schools where we have offered staff coaching there has been very positive feedback and the following points highlighted:

- The service is short term, on-site, and easily accessible (although some schools in our experience have also valued the opportunity for staff to access coaching sessions off-site, for reasons of confidentiality within staff teams).
- After having experienced SFBC some staff found it useful to use SF skills to informally support colleagues.
- Staff who accessed SFBC for themselves found that they were more likely to make use of the student SFBC service for their students.
- Staff who accessed SFBC found it useful to use SF skills with their tutees.

Examples of staff feedback about coaching

I found the sessions really helpful, I liked the positive approach and the looking at my strengths, it gave me clarity and focus.

The sessions allowed me time to reflect, think out loud, remember what I want and put my thoughts into action. I have recommended the sessions to other staff.

The sessions expanded my vision of reaching my goals, in fact I have changed my attitude to my goals.

Case examples

Saidah: The shortness of life and the possibility of everything . . .

Saidah was a girl who had joined the school in Year 10 from her home in the North East of Africa, having come to live with her family in this country. Saidah was coming for coaching sessions both at her own request and by school referral because she felt she was struggling with the work. For many students, attending lessons and being able to learn is a complex business, and it is an emotional as well as an educational journey.

In our first session I asked Saidah what her best hopes from the coaching were and she said she wanted to find a way to feel better about her school work. She wanted to feel more positive, and to be able to think 'I am going to pass my subjects', instead of feeling 'what's the point, I am going to fail anyway'. I asked her how she would know she was feeling more positive, and she said she would be going to all her lessons instead of missing some, keeping up with her course work and meeting her deadlines. She described this as 'giving myself my best chance'. We explored why this was important to her. She wanted to do well for her family and for herself because she wanted a good career.

For most of the rest of the session I asked Saidah more about 'giving myself the best chance'. She wanted to ask for help from teachers or other students, talk more in class, and not be put off by mistakes. She noticed that she was doing some of these things already. She had asked for help once recently, she had talked more in a class and she had tried to carry on with some work after making some mistakes. On a scale, where 10 was giving herself her best chance and 0 the opposite, she put herself at 3. More questions about why she was there and not lower turned up the fact that she had joined the local library recently and that she was speaking a bit more to teachers, even if it was just to say 'I don't know'.

In subsequent sessions we explored more of Saidah's progress. She started to improve her lesson attendance and to do things a bit differently in lessons, in her work and in her interactions with others. Some students began to ask her for help which enabled her to talk more and to feel she could do the work. She also began to sit closer to the other students, and to ask them things too. Asking what others had noticed was fruitful as she described how people were beginning to see 'more' of her.

By the fourth session Saidah thought she was on a 9 on her scale. She was talking and sharing ideas more, and keeping going when she made mistakes; for example, even if she answered a teacher's question and it was the wrong answer she felt OK, and she was happy to redo a piece of coursework at her teacher's request; she saw this as on the way to giving herself her best chance rather than as an example of failure. I asked her who was least surprised at all the changes she had made and the answer was her aunt, who had known her from a young child, and 'she knows I have it in me'. Saidah said other people were starting to see what she had in her too.

Saidah had plenty of ideas in her final session about how she would know when she had reached 10 on her scale, which was where she wanted to be. I asked her what she knew about herself that made her confident that she would reach her 10. She said she was someone who could carry on trying, and was not scared to try. She was also someone who liked herself and was 'open to others' and she had noticed that these two things had made a big difference to her work. She said: 'I was closed before, now I'm happy. I used to think people didn't like me but now when I look back I think I didn't like myself'.

Finally I asked her what advice she would give to another student who might be in a similar situation to the one she had been:

'Life is too short. Love yourself. Nothing is impossible.'

Keni: Walking in a different way . . .

Keni was a boy referred for coaching in Year 8 because of the number of fights he was getting into. He experienced other students as picking on him and making his life unhappy and would become very angry and lash out. Keni had many ambitions: he wanted to be famous and to run a hotel. He wanted to get some good exam passes, earn money and buy smart clothes. The school wanted him to manage his anger. Keni's best hopes from the coaching were to get on better at school so that he could achieve his ambitions. We looked at what sort of life he wanted for himself in school which would help him on his way to the sort of life he wanted outside school. I encouraged him to describe this in detail. It included taking part more in his lessons, ignoring other students' negative comments, walking in a different way around the school, smiling and starting conversations, and playing basketball more with others. I asked Keni to show me what he meant by some of these descriptions. He was good at drama and so he role-played talking, smiling, focusing, answering questions and especially walking in a different way around my room.

When we scaled how things were Keni noticed that he had been focusing more in one class recently and he had talked a bit more with other students in another class. In subsequent sessions he continued to surprise himself and to notice things he had already done which were part of how he wanted his life to be in school. When I asked Keni what these changes told him about himself he said that he could see that he was a person who walked differently around the school. He thought maybe he could get on with others, be in a team, maybe even lead a team when he was older. He told me that when he was in Year 7 he thought 'relationships are not for me', now he was considering thinking of making more social contact with other students outside school. He continued to ignore negative comments or annoying actions from other students, keeping himself calm and avoiding fights most of the time. Instead he was trying to focus on his work, and on talking more with other students. These things were important to Keni, they were about having the life he wanted to have, and they included, but were not confined to, managing his anger. After the first few sessions, I saw Keni at intermittent intervals whenever he or the school decided it might be helpful. He continued to report that things were slowly getting better. There were one or two setbacks, when he became angry in the playground, but he did not let these incidents take any hold in his life. He continued to walk around the school in a different way.

The school had wanted Keni to manage his anger, and this was achieved to some degree, not by any focus on 'anger', or indeed on 'keeping calm', but by helping him to describe the sort of life he wanted in school.

References

Ajmal, Y. and Rees, I. (Eds) (2001) *Solution in Schools: Creative Applications of Solution Focused Brief Thinking with Young People and Adults*. London: BT Press.

Berg, I.K. and Shilts, L. (2005) Keeping the solutions inside the classroom. *ASCA School Counselor* July/August.

de Shazer, S. (1994) *Words Were Originally Magic*. New York: W.W. Norton.

Hillel, V. and Smith, E. (2001) Empowering students to empower others. In Ajmal, Y. and Rees, I. (Eds) (2001) *Solution in Schools: Creative Applications of Solution Focused Brief Thinking with Young People and Adults*. London: BT Press.

Kelly, M., Kim, J. and Franklin, C. (2008) *Solution Focused Brief Therapy in Schools: A 360-degree View of Research & Practice*. Oxford: Oxford University Press.

Korman, H. (2004) *The Common Project* (available at www.sikt.nu).

Lee, M.Y., Sebold, J. and Uken, A. (2003) *Solution-Focused Treatment of Domestic Violence Offenders: Accountability for Change*. Oxford: Oxford University Press.

Mahlberg, K. and Sjoblom, M. (2004) Solution focused education. http://www.fkc.se.

Metcalf, L. (2008) *Counselling Towards Solutions: A Practical, Solution-Focused Program for Working with Students, Teachers and Parents*, 2nd ed. San Francisco: Jossey-Bass.

Ratner, H., George, E. and Iveson, C. (2012) *Solution Focused Brief Therapy: 100 Key points and Techniques*. London: Routledge.

Rhodes, J. and Ajmal, Y. (1995) *Solution Focused Thinking in Schools*. London: BT Press.

Shilts, L. (2013) The WOWW Programme. In De Jong, P. and Berg, I.K. (Eds) *Interviewing for Solutions*, 4th ed. Pacific Grove, CA: Brooks/Cole.

Young, S. (2009) *Solution-Focused Schools: Anti-Bullying and Beyond*. London: BT Press.

Chapter 7

In different settings

The context

Coaches can be involved in coaching children and young people in a variety of different settings, other than schools. Apart from private practice, coaches could be working in statutory or voluntary projects and in alternative and higher education.

In every setting it is important to make sure that the coach's contract with the young person fits with the job the coach has been asked to do in the organisation. This is often simpler to negotiate in schools, where staff are used to having different external professionals coming in to work with them; it may be different working for a small voluntary organisation or project. Using an SF structure in initial discussions can help to clarify processes, outcomes and boundaries. For example, it can be useful to ask about the hopes of the organisation from the coaching and how the organisation will know that these hopes are being achieved. Confidentiality about the client content of sessions can be discussed and agreed, and it is useful to meet with someone regularly to check that the coaching is on target for the organisation, discuss aspects which are working well, and decide on any improvements that are necessary.

Solution Focused Brief Coaching (SFBC) is straightforward in its structure and does not refer to complex theories of psychological development or complex ideas about change processes. This means that staff in organisations where coaches work do not experience any sense of exclusion from the coaching process, as the purpose and nature of the coaching conversations are accessible to all. This can help to ensure that the coaching service provided is fully connected to the organisation and not just an add-on service. Sometimes young people involved in coaching sessions are happy to meet other staff members of the organisation to give feedback on what they are doing in coaching, or to report their particular achievements. It is important to respect the wishes of the young person regarding privacy, and some young people may prefer to keep their sessions confidential.

The fit

The simple and straightforward nature of SFBC means that it is able to fit and flow with many different working contexts The short-term, resource-based and future-focus of the approach has made it useful not only in the cost-cutting statutory sectors, and where services are privatised, but also in the voluntary, small business and charitable sectors, where more pared-down, innovative and shorter-term approaches have had a long history of success. Placing the customer at the centre of the work, in a respectful and authentic way, is important to most enterprises, and SFBC fits this requirement because of its invitation to the client to look ahead to the life that they aspire to, and to identify their own unique ways of getting there.

Areas of application

The client-centredness of the SF model and lack of assessment criteria mean that it can work with a range of issues in widely varying contexts. Some examples include: foster carers who have used SF coaching skills with their foster children and in meetings and reviews; residential workers (Durrant 1993); and substance-misuse workers, who have a long history of using the SF approach effectively in their work, including with young people (Berg & Miller 1992; Berg and Reuss 1997). There is also increasing interest in the use of SF coaching skills for phone, email and online support services for young people, utilising their communication tools of choice. The SFBC model in all of these contexts will remain consistent in its structure, although some types of SF question may be favoured above others. It is the clients who create the differences, in the content and life they bring to the session.

Three examples of where I have used SFBC in other settings have been in (1) a charity working with children, young people and adults who are living with conditions affecting their appearance; (2) a charity advising families whose children are involved with statutory children's services; and (3) a charity working with disaffected and vulnerable young people through a physical and artistic activity.

Charity 1

This charity offers practical and emotional support to families and individuals where there is a member who has a condition affecting their appearance, and they also offer training to education and health agencies and have a campaigning role. I worked in their children and young people's service, where support sessions are offered to individuals face-to-face and on the telephone as part of a package of support, which includes other services such as information, workshops, groups and peer support.

Families contacted this charity or were referred for different reasons. It might be a family who had a new baby with a visible physical difference, or parents concerned about how their child would talk about their difference when starting a new school. It might be a teenager wanting to manage their appearance in a more confident and independent way. Key elements in all the services provided included respecting families' past experiences, helping families to identify their strengths and resources, and supporting families to develop positive ideas about their futures. SFBC therefore fitted well into this organisation.

During sessions, parents talked about wanting to be sure that they were doing the right things for their child, about how to model confident conversations about difference to their children, and about handling others' reactions. Young people talked about going out and meeting people rather than hiding away, about fears as well as hopes for their future, and about managing people's comments and questions in a positive way. As they talked about future successes which they hoped for, they also often began to recognise instances of past success. Experiences of difficulty and challenge, of which there were many, also became an opportunity to explore the strengths and resources they had drawn on. In this way, SFBC could help families, children and young people affected by physical differences to begin to envisage and move towards the life that they wanted, and to draw on the difficulties and challenges they had experienced, as a resource for their present and future life.

The services at this charity led to change on multiple levels. For example, raising the public profile of issues often helped individuals to feel more confident, and work with individuals often led them to raise the profile of the issues in their own environments. In this way, change starts to snowball in different directions. SFBC can have this effect too; clients talk about and begin to inhabit a small part of the life that they want in a session; then they go ahead alone, changing their own lives and those of others around them.

Charity 2

My second example is a charity advising and supporting families whose children are involved with, or need, children's services. I worked in one of their advocacy projects supporting parents attending conferences concerned with child protection, family support or child reviews. My previous experience as a social worker in child protection and family support enabled me to provide specialist knowledge of child protection and local authority processes, and my SF coaching skills helped me to empower parents to express their voice.

Many of the parents I worked with were young people who spoke of their anxiety and worries about parenting and about being judged. Their best hopes from our sessions often included being able to speak up in conferences and to be able to communicate and demonstrate that they had made changes in their lives and could keep their child safe and well in the future. I invited them to tell me about this future, in as much detail as possible, and they talked about the sort of family life they wanted to create for their child, and their ambitions for themselves, to go to college and to find a career. Each young person's vision, and description, was unique to them, and it was in the process of describing this life that the young person seemed literally to start to inhabit that space. They began to recognise the things that they were already doing which were making that life happen, and to see themselves in a more confident way. This recognition helped them to do themselves justice in the conference, and on many occasions my work as an advocate was confined to a coaching session before the conference.

Charity 3

My third example is that of providing a coaching service within a charity working with persistent young offenders, vulnerable young people, and young people at risk or disconnected from education, employment and often their families. Many have experienced homelessness, abuse, the care system, the courts, and sometimes prison. The charity's mission is to release the potential of young people who experience marginalisation and alienation through their engagement with carefully planned, tightly focused and highly disciplined artistic activity programmes.

Young people are offered challenging targets during the programmes and intensive support to achieve them. Individual coaching sessions have also been available on some of the programmes, where young people can think about their hopes and aspirations for themselves during the programme or in their life outside. Many students have wanted to talk about feeling more confident about themselves, and what this meant to each of them was very different. Students have often described what might seem to be very small, simple steps. But to these young people, often from lives which involved gangs, violence, loss, and disconnections from significant relationships, simple does not mean easy. It is so often the case in the West that we mistake simple for easy and complex for difficult (Iles 2013). These young people never seemed to make this mistake. They often described to me their hopes and wishes in simple, clear terms and helped me to understand how challenging they were too. One student described wanting to be able to start conversations with others and would notice himself sitting a bit closer to other students at break times and taking his headphones off. Another student talked about going to the front rather than the back of the rehearsal room for a change, and not feeling afraid when people looked at him. Many talked about taking more risks and trying things more, or about being able to talk seriously in front of people 'and not just be the one with the jokes'. Students wanted to feel more positive about their lives; one student said she would know this because she would stop listening to slow depressive music, eat more and be able to say 'no' when she wanted to. A student said during a coaching session that she had realised 'you can't wait until you feel better before you do something, you have to do something to feel better'.

During the programme students experience themselves doing things that they would not have thought possible before. On their journey to these achievements students find themselves recognising their resources, sometimes for the first time in their lives, and making the tiny changes which together weave a new story about them. These things can be very small to an outside observer but very significant to the young person. One girl told me during the coaching that she had taken more risks. When I asked her about this she said she hated her feet but she had learnt to take her socks off in the activity class, first at the back of the room and later at the front. This had been a huge achievement for her. Other young people were taking other risks: being more energetic in the studio, hanging out a bit more with other students at the end of the day, beginning to trust other young people enough to work with them, and as one said, 'showing myself more, not just an act', not a new story then, just one which had been hidden from view.

Students also talked in coaching about wanting to stay in charge of themselves, ignore the provocations from others ('I'm learning to ignore others, and push my boundaries not theirs'), trying to make their own decisions out on the streets, talking to people in a different way ('helping people to be less scared of me so then I can be more friendly with them'), or just staying 'low key'. Some students wanted to talk about keeping themselves calm enough to get on with the things they wanted to do; for others it was important to talk about when they would know it was right to move on from the anger they felt about some of the things that had happened to them. The future focus of SFBC was very important to these young people, many of whom had experienced numerous services coming into their lives. One girl told me at the start of coaching 'I've had a difficult life but I want to be able to talk about a future'. Another said 'I am sick of talking about what went wrong in my life. I've done that. If you want to ask questions about that I'm leaving'. She stayed.

Making lists was a useful coaching tool with many young people, encouraging them to recognise small signs of success, such as 20 things a girl had been pleased with herself for taking more part in the programme, and 25 things a boy would notice about himself that told him he was taking good risks rather than bad ones. Lists of what others had or would notice about the young person often seemed powerful, and helped to develop positive relationship experiences for the young person. For example, I asked for 10 things that the dedicated hostel worker found inspiring about working with them, 20 reasons why prison officers believed they would not see a particular young person return to prison again, 15 things a girl's friends appreciated about her, and 10 people who had cared about a girl in her past and present (she got to 15).

I found it useful to employ coaching materials with some of the young people: coaching cards where they could record their best hopes and their resources and achievements. I also used top tip cards from other young people and invited them to contribute to these too (Chapter 8).

The young people were beginning to explore new stories about themselves, stories which they could see were not transient acts in their lives but which had pathways from their past and into their future, and connected to the relationships around them. These stories were constructed and developed through a combination of factors in this charity: through the medium and metaphor of their artistic activity programme, and through the power of language in SFBC. Their activity, their words, their worlds.

Young people talking in coaching sessions

I am putting more effort in and this is making me feel less tired not more tired.

I let someone else on the bus first, this is me showing more respect.

I'm going to carry on saying 'I can do that'.

Now I know I can be a good person . . . people do like me and I'm not bad.

I learnt I can work hard, even go through my fear.

I'm not going back to doing nothing, being in bed, being tired, not feeling confident.

This is how I'm thinking now: I am strong, some things get me down . . . then I get up.

By the third day I thought I don't want to do this. It's not for me. I might as well stop now. That's how I used to think. Now I think different. More things might be for me.

I thought a lot of things made me look stupid. Now I know not all things make me look stupid, and maybe it's even me who thinks I look stupid and not other people.

I've dropped out of a lot of things because when I looked ahead I thought I wasn't the sort of person who could finish those things. Now I'm thinking different.

Case studies

Samia 'A new bag'

Samia was a 16-year-old girl who was referred to the third charity by her social worker. She was living away from home and had experienced many difficulties and challenges in her life.

Samia told me that she usually tried to wrap up her thoughts in a bag and ignore them – but that it was difficult to do this. The thoughts were often very self-critical, and she wanted to be less harsh towards herself, believe in herself more, and not give up on herself all the time – to have a different bag of thoughts perhaps. The difference this would make for her was that she would feel more confident and perhaps do some things in other ways, and this became our contract of work. I asked her what sorts of things she might notice the next morning when she woke up if she were more confident and doing things differently. Some of her ideas included:

- Looking in the mirror first thing and smiling
- Holding up her head on the bus
- Going to the front or at least to the middle of the rehearsal room, and not straight to the back
- Being in a positive mood and spreading this around by making jokes, or being nice to other people
- Focusing more on the activity, and staying in the lesson even if she was finding something difficult
- Sitting closer to other people at lunchtimes
- Taking her headphones out sometimes when with other people

We talked more about this day, about how other people would respond to her and about how she would react to this. During this conversation there were some very small things she recognised that she had already been doing, such as sitting a bit closer to other students and not storming out of the studio so often. We explored these instances, how she had done them, and how others had reacted; for example, one or two students included her in conversations when she was sitting nearer and other people had offered to help her when she stayed in the studio.

On a scale of 0 to 10 – where 10 was Samia being more confident and doing things in the different way that she wanted to, and 0 was the opposite – she put herself at 1.5. When I asked her how she knew she was there and not lower, she said she knew she was at least 1.5 because of the instances above. I asked her what else told her she was at 1.5. She thought a bit and then said she had at least looked in the mirror this morning, though she had not smiled at herself. When I asked her 'what else' again she thought for quite a while, then said 'because I know that Samia is in here somewhere, she's just hidden'. I think this was an interesting example of using the SF question 'what else' to help the client to recognise their resources, instances of success and hope that are often very hard to see. Signs of moving up the scale were Samia noticing herself not giving up so quickly, keep trying things, and thinking of mistakes as mistakes and not the whole story about her.

At the end of this session Samia said that she didn't realise what being confident looked like until she started talking about it. Hearing herself describe it in detail had helped her to see it as a possibility, to begin to move around in this vision, and to experience some parts of it already happening.

In the second and third sessions, Samia had noticed some further small changes. She had been able to look in her mirror and smile at herself when she got up, and she had also been able to look more at herself in the studio mirrors. This had been helping her to try more in the studio and to stay when things were challenging. Other people, staff and students, had noticed these changes, and because of the intensity of the programme, there were continual opportunities to practice small changes, so that they could develop rather than lose their lustre. Samia felt she could continue to develop her confidence and her different way of doing things when she left the programme. She had great hopes for herself in the future, and different ideas about the sorts of jobs which she might do. In short, she had stopped giving up on herself. This was both a good place to be when she finished the programme and a fantastic place to start.

Shayne 'Cutting out the bacon'

Shayne was a 17-year-old boy who had arrived at the third charity via a route which had included dropping out of college and offending behaviour. He lived at home and was trying to move away from some of the gang relationships he had on the street.

Shayne's best hopes from coaching were to be able to make the most of being at the charity. He said he usually dropped out of things when they got difficult. His first few days on the programme had made him feel it was not for him, so he had thought he might as well stop coming. Every day when he cooked himself a bacon breakfast he found himself thinking there was no point in hurrying the bacon because there was no point in coming to the charity. However, the staff team at the charity never let go of students easily, and although he continued to come very late or not at all, they kept in contact with him, and encouraged and supported and persuaded him to keep trying. Shayne found himself connecting more to the programme and took up a number of coaching sessions.

Shayne wanted to make the most of his time on the programme, and making a success of being there. This was our contract for coaching. I asked Shayne what he would be noticing when he was making a success of being on the programme. He described a number of things:

* Getting up on time, eating cereal and cutting out the bacon, and getting to the studio on time
* Going to bed when he was tired, at midnight or earlier
* Doing some of the things he was scared of doing in the programme
* Turning his head away from any disruptive behaviour in the studio
* Being respectful to the tutors, answering questions or at least acknowledging their questions
* Putting in effort and doing his best, not half his best
* Talking more to other students in free time, volunteering comments or starting conversations
* Assuming students talking about him were positive or neutral, not negative (unless proved otherwise)

We talked about how much of this behaviour was about taking risks, and Shayne said he had seen himself as a risk taker in the past, but the risks he was facing now, doing the things he was scared of doing on the programme, were harder to take. However, thinking about himself as someone who was able to take risks was important for him to remember, as opposed to thinking about himself as someone who dropped out when things got difficult. Perhaps they were different sides of the same behaviour too: Shayne could stick at things (not drop out) by continuing to take risks.

In the second session Shayne reported proudly that he had 'cut the bacon'. This had not been easy but he had done it. Everything about being on time had flowed from this for him: he had managed the earlier nights, and negotiating a complex London transport journey held no difficulties for him. We explored at length how he had done this. One of the things he had noticed was that, when he woke up in the morning, he was thinking about his skills in risk taking (going to the programme) and not about his history of dropping out. I asked him who had noticed this, and he said his mum had commented 'What's wrong with you?' in a jokey way. This had made him laugh and it had led to a 'good atmosphere' in the house, which had made him feel even more energetic. I asked him what else he had noticed was different. He said he hadn't been joining in disruptions in the studio and had not even needed to turn his head to do this. I asked him what difference this had made to the other students and he said that one or two had asked him 'What's up?' and he had said 'I want to do stuff on the programme'. To his surprise they had agreed with him about doing this too, and this made him feel good. I wondered what this told him about himself and he said he thought maybe he could be a bit of a leader. I asked him what else was different. After a time Shayne said he realised that things had started to be a bit different for him on the streets a while back, he was staying friends with people but turning his head away from certain activities. This was something he had already been doing but hadn't noticed.

In further sessions I continued to explore with Shayne what he was doing to make a success for himself of his time on the programme. He continued to have some difficult days and difficult times but he also continued to make a lot of effort. When I asked him who else saw him making a success, the most powerful comment for him came from an old friend: he had been talking about how hard he was working on the programme to this friend, who had responded 'That sounds like a job!'. Shayne had never had a job.

At the end of the programme Shayne felt that he had made a success of his time there, and this was partly defined by the effort he had seen himself put in. It was also defined by the difference putting an effort in made for Shayne. He told me one of the most important things he had realised was 'Just because I don't like something the first time doesn't mean it's not for me. Maybe there's even more things for me than I thought'. Success for him was also beginning to have a different story to tell himself and to show others. And, as he said, it had started with cutting out the bacon.

References

Berg, I.K. and Miller, S.D. (1992) *Working With the Problem Drinker: A Solution Focused Approach*. New York: W.W. Norton.

Berg, I.K. and Reuss, N. (1997) *Solutions Step By Step: A Substance Abuse Treatment Manual*. New York: Norton and Wylie.

Durrant, M. (1993) *A Cooperative, Competency Based Approach to Therapy and Program Design*. New York: W.W. Norton.

Iles, V. (2013) Mindful Coaching: Focusing on the 'Simple Hard' Instead of the 'Complicated Easy'. Presentation for Association For Coaches, 30 October, London.

Chapter 8

Materials

Throughout this book we have made reference to the use of materials in Solution Focused Brief Coaching (SFBC) with children and young people. In this chapter I will try to draw some of the ideas together to give you some examples of materials you might use in your work, and perhaps encourage you to develop and use your own materials if you are not already doing so. Coaches who design materials during a session with a child or young person, rather than bringing materials into the sessions, are often able to stay close to the child or young person's conversation – for example, drawing a scale which particularly suits the child's ideas or aspirations. This also means that materials do not have to be elaborate or expensive. However, sometimes it can be helpful to have some ideas for materials in your mind, or some actual materials to hand if the need arises, or you may want to plan a coaching programme which includes particular materials.

Why use materials?

SFBC is about having conversations. Conversations can, and often do, work well on their own with children and young people. Words have a magical element to many children, and the Miracle Question (or 'magic wand' for the youngest!), for example, may not require so much of a leap of faith for children and young people as it might with adults. Children also learn to make sense of the world through imaginative play, and so non-verbal means of communication can be a good support and extension for conversation. This is especially true for younger children who are still developing their language skills.

Some children and teenagers just do not find talking easy, particularly if it is with adults or professionals or those outside the circle of family and friends. Others may have a short attention span so that talking becomes boring or difficult to attend to, and still others may have a lot of energy – so more physical ways of communicating will help them to stay focused.

How to use materials

It is important to make sure that any materials are used as an integral part of the SFBC process and not as stand-alone or random activities. They are a communication tool used to enhance rather than replace conversation. They can be informal or planned, occasional or routine, but always guided by the needs of the child or young person. We see them as providing additional ways of looking at, seeing, remembering, expanding, re-describing, including, firming up, finding out, and celebrating.

Using materials in this approach is not a way for the practitioner to interpret, understand 'what is really going on', or assess the child. The materials are simply a means of helping the child articulate hopes, describe possible ways forward, and highlight achievements. Rather than try to 'look beneath' we stay as close as we can to the child we see and hear. We call this 'staying on the surface'.

Materials can be used at any stage of the work. 'Strength cards', for instance, may be used at the beginning of sessions to focus on and celebrate a child's own strengths and skills and to start the session in a positive way. The child's hopes may be drawn or written and recorded on a small 'coaching card'. Preferred futures can be drawn, made into a list, or written out on a mind map. Scales can be drawn out in the session or pre-made, or use can be made of the surroundings as a scale. Small signs of anticipatory progress can be recorded on a coaching card, as can signs of progress made. Small 'credit cards' can be given to the child by themselves and given to others who have been helping them. Small 'quote cards' can be made by children and young people to advise and support themselves and other children. Lists, drawings, mind maps (see below) and coaching cards can be used throughout sessions to help explore progress, others' perspectives, ideas about what to do (strategies), and ideas about the sort of person you are (identity). Materials like these are not so much used as a record but as a dynamic part of the session, helping the child or young person to explore, remember and anticipate.

You can find materials in many places. There is the environment around you in the session, the environment nearby (such as taking an 'SF walk' – see Chapter 2 – or scaling using the natural environment), materials you have to hand or easily available (such as paper, crayons, toys), materials you create in the session or create yourself before your sessions, and the materials other people have created. Some materials are specifically designed for SF work, others are materials which can be used in an SF way. When you have found something which works, share it!

Examples of materials

Strengths and resources

Strength cards, with different qualities and skills on each card, are available from many different companies and sources. One of the best sets I have used is from St Lukes' Innovative Resources (St Lukes' Innovative Resources: www.innovative resources.org), who have many different packs and materials for children and teenagers of different ages. They usually consist of around 30 brightly coloured cards with simple words and pictures depicting qualities such as kindness, honesty, courage and loyalty (or activities and questions related to these qualities). Sometimes I have these spread on the table or the floor during a session, and the child or young person might choose to use them during the session to 'remember' qualities or skills they have. Sometimes I use them at the beginning of a session, to think about skills and strengths they have, by way of an introduction. In subsequent sessions I might use them at the beginning of the session to find out which quality or qualities they have used since the last session, or were most pleased about using, and which one they want to notice themselves using more of before the next session. Even sorting through the pack can help to remind children and young people of their many different skills and strengths. This is usually tied in to whatever they are working on in the session. There are many more ways to employ these cards in your practice: for example, what qualities do the child's friends, family, or teachers most appreciate about them, or what would they be most pleased to see them using. Children and young people can also ask a friend or family member or teacher to look out for them – and compliment them for – using a particular skill or quality.

A more personal way to highlight a child's qualities adapts an idea of Matthew Selekman to provide a visual 'identity' description of the child (Selekman 1997). Draw an outline of the child on a large piece of paper (flipchart paper and sellotape will do the trick) and pass a magic wand or magic machine over the outline in order to show up all the child's different resources and skills.

Coaching cards

Coaching cards can be bought but they are not difficult to make with card, scissors and crayons – and if you want to use them a lot, a small laminating machine is a good investment. Home-made cards have the advantage of fitting more exactly with your way of working and the issues your clients face. They can be related to school, family or friends or to typical life-cycle events such as changing school or divorcing parents. You can make them at home or co-produce them with each child – certainly children enjoy this process, especially if stickers are available to supplement the 'art work'. Below, I mention some of the cards I use. Finally, as children often like to help their friends, I have created some 'top tip' cards to encourage children and young people to share their ideas with their peers. When a child reports a success or achievement we will see if it can be generalised into a top tip. As well as consolidating the child's success this helps to create an atmosphere of cooperation and inclusion in schools and other settings.

Example 1: Coaching cards

Credit cards: 'Best hopes', 'Thank you', 'Well done', 'Keep doing' (see Figures 8.1 to 8.4, respectively).

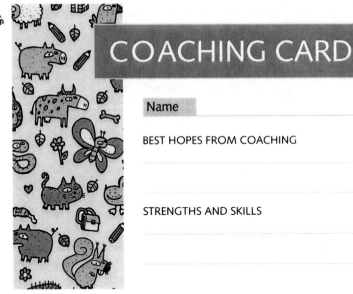

COACHING CARD

Name

BEST HOPES FROM COACHING

STRENGTHS AND SKILLS

Figure 8.1

COACHING CARD

CREDIT

Name

THANK YOU FOR...

Figure 8.2

Figure 8.3

Figure 8.4

Top tip card: 'Don't change for other people, change for yourself' (see Figure 8.5).

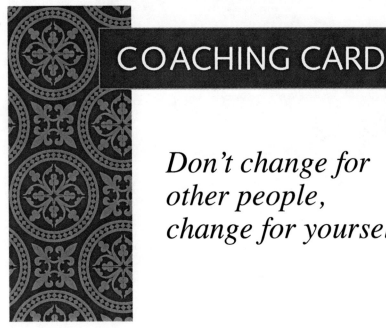

COACHING CARD

Don't change for other people, change for yourself

Figure 8.5

Scales

Scales can be constructed using many different forms, and not just with numbers. Mostly they will be drawn (or constructed) in the session, but pre-prepared scales can also be useful when they connect to a child's particular interests: downward-directed scales can be helpful, such as ski slopes for older children and slides for younger ones. Upward scales might suit those who relish difficult challenges, and sports-related scales might provide a measure for other aspects of life: a scale made up of increasingly difficult skateboard or dance manoeuvres, for instance. Straight roads and winding paths, stairways, ladders and mountains – the possibilities become endless when a commitment is made to see each child as unique. St Lukes produces a pack of pads with a variety of scales drawn out; they are ready to use. I also have a large home-made laminated scale which children enjoy using. For more active fun I sometimes use 'jumping scales' – numbered pieces of paper spread out so that the child has to jump to their chosen place. Older children or teenagers may prefer a scale which is unique to them, and thus confidential. Scales can also be made in the room in which you are working, using something to mark the ground, or in the outside area using the natural materials or plants which are there.

Sometimes I give children small laminated scales and stickers to take away and they can keep a record of where they are on the scale. The scale usually comes back covered in stickers because positions often change from day to day. Recognising this helps children to feel more optimistic about possibilities, and you can talk about the highest point they reached in the last few days/week/month.

Example 2: Scales

These include small numbered scales (see Figure 8.6) and picture scales (see Figure 8.7).

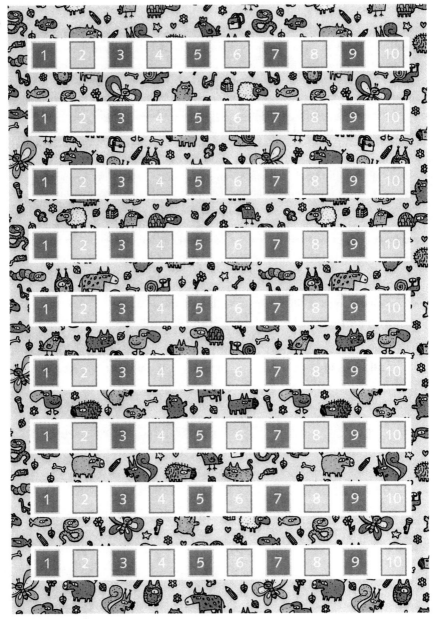

Figure 8.6

Figure 8.7

Lists

Making lists with children and young people can have many benefits, including helping the child or young person to find more examples of whatever you are both looking for. A long list seems to make it easier for them to find things to add, perhaps because it suggests a more arbitrary nature to the contents (I can add less serious items if I am looking for 20 things than if I am looking for 3 things). It also helps children and young people to come up with things which are sometimes more useful to them precisely because they are less visible to them, and they have had to think about them; and finally, I think that a pre-made list, or even a list just written up to the 20 or 30 mark before you start, has a motivating effect on the child or young person. They can see the numbers there and they can see how they get filled up, a similar effect to seeing or imagining a scale.

I use a variety of list resources in my work, including numbered and unspecified lists, lists which include best hopes and preferred futures, lists of what went well, and lists of what is worth looking out for etc.

Example 3: Lists

These include: 'A person who believes in me: list of reasons' (see Figure 8.8), 'Best hopes, and list of what this will look like' (see Figure 8.9), and 'List of what went well' (see Figure 8.10).

A PERSON WHO BELIEVES I CAN SUCCEED IS...

_____

THIS IS WHY THIS PERSON BELIEVES THAT I CAN SUCCEED:

1 _____

2 _____

3 _____

4 _____

5 _____

6 _____

7 _____

8 _____

9 _____

10 _____

THINGS THAT WILL MAKE MORE PEOPLE BELIEVE I CAN SUCCEED:

1 _____

2 _____

3 _____

4 _____

5 _____

Figure 8.8

eRESOURCES

BEST HOPES FROM COACHING

WHAT WILL THIS LOOK LIKE AND WHAT DIFFERENCE WILL IT MAKE?

1
2
3
4
5
6
7
8
9
10

SCALE

1 5 10

NOTICE NEXT WEEK

1
2
3
4
5

Figure 8.9

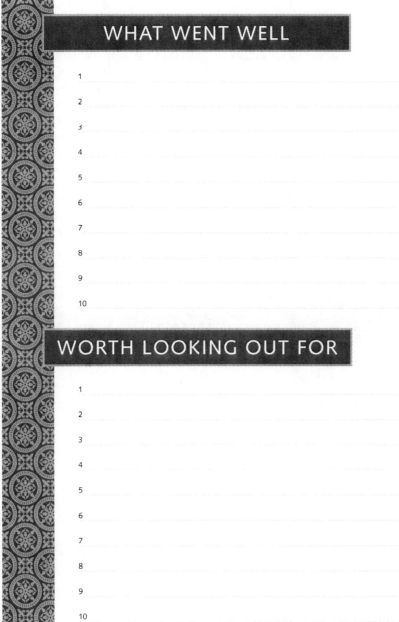

WHAT WENT WELL

1
2
3
4
5
6
7
8
9
10

WORTH LOOKING OUT FOR

1
2
3
4
5
6
7
8
9
10

Figure 8.10

Mind maps

Mind maps are visual diagrams of a central idea – around which grow many other smaller ideas, like a map of a city with roads spread around in all directions, or a roman candle spreading out in the sky from the initial burst of light. Mind maps can provide a function similar to that of lists, but they can also help children and young people to find, organise and remember material. I think that they are particularly appropriate to use in SFBC because of their capacity to catch and record ideas and thoughts which might not seem immediately relevant. As Tony Buzan says, 'Start in the centre of a blank page turned sideways. Why? Because starting in the centre gives your brain freedom to spread out in all directions and to express itself more freely and naturally' (Buzan 2005: 17). I often use a form of mind map for many different purposes – to explore strengths and skills, to talk about best hopes and preferred futures, to talk about progress made, and to think about other person perspectives etc. The main idea can be written in the centre, and more outward roads or spines added if needed. Sometimes children are quite eager to take mind maps away with them to fill in with all the things they are noticing in between sessions.

Example 4: Mind maps

These include: the 'Being more confident' mind map (see Figure 8.11) and the 'What's been better for me' mind map (see Figure 8.12).

Figure 8.11

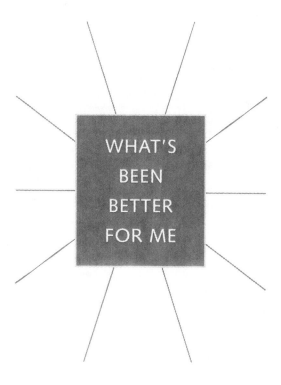

WHAT'S BEEN BETTER FOR ME

Figure 8.12

Forms

When working with young people I sometimes use a Solution Focused form which they can take away if they would like a record of the meeting. Teenagers can forget things, or can be dealing with a lot of information and issues coming at them from different sources and devices; some teenagers have told me that a simple brief record of their session is helpful. It does not stop the work going on in their head and their heart. These sorts of form, when blank, can be given to other agencies you are working in to show them the sort of work you will be doing too. With young people, texts and emails can be used for the same purpose if this is helpful and has been agreed with the referral agency or work setting.

Example 5: Record forms

These include: the 'Coaching record form' (see Figure 8.13) and the 'Coaching project session record and prompt form' (see Figure 8.14).

eRESOURCES

COACHING PROGRAMME

COACHING RECORD FORM

Name Session No./Date Age

Background to coaching session (e.g. organisation/private, referred or self request)

Strengths Skills Resources

Best Hopes From Coaching

Preferred Future Details

Instances and Exceptions

What's Been Better (2nd and subsequent sessions)

Scales

A thought/idea you want to take from this session

Compliments

Invitation to watch out for signs of moving up the scale

Figure 8.13

COACHING PROJECT

COACHING SESSION RECORD/GUIDE

Name

1 **Introductions, refreshments questions**

2 **Strength and skills**

STRENGTHS CARDS Choose your favourites about yourself, and ones you'd like to practice more.

Who is a best friend for you? What would this friend say you are good at/appreciates about you ?

What would your teachers and parents say you are good at/appreciate about you?

What does your pet think you are good at/appreciate about you ?

What do YOU think you are good at/appreciate about yourself ?

What else do you think you are good at/appreciate about yourself ?

What is it about you that makes you good at this/these things ?

3 **Best hopes**

What are your best hopes from coaching?
What would you like to get better at, change or do differently? How would it be good for you if you got better at this? What difference would it make?
What would your teacher's best hopes be from coaching?
What would your parent/carer's best hopes be from coaching?

4 **Preferred future**

Imagine that tonight, when you go to sleep, a miracle happens
Imagine tomorrow when you wake up things are going better for you in the way that you want. What will be the first tiny sign that things are different….and the next…and the next…..(through the day)
What will you be doing? How will others respond to that? Then how will you respond? What will that tell you about yourself?

Who will be the first person to notice something is different? What will they see?

Who won't be surprised to see something different? What do they know about you which means they knew you could do this?

What will your friends notice?

What would your parents and teachers notice?

Figure 8.14 (continued on page 138)

COACHING PROJECT

COACHING SESSION RECORD/GUIDE

5   Instances and exceptions

When have you noticed yourself doing some of these things?
When have other people noticed some of these things?
What have you done which is already helping towards getting better at these things?
What does that tell you about yourself?

6   Scaling (progress)

On a scale of 1 to 10 where 10 is that things are going really well in the way that you want and 1 is the opposite

- Where are you now?

- What tells you that you are there and not at the number below? What else? what else? what else? Where would your parent or teacher or friend put you? How would they know?

- Let's imagine you move 1 point up the scale, how will you know? What signs might you notice which will tell you? What might other people notice?

How confident are you about moving up the scale? 10 is you know you can definitely do it and 1 is you are not sure at all.

- What do you know about yourself which tells you that you can be that confident about this?

How committed are you to moving up the scale? 10 is you'll do anything it takes, 1 you don't much care.

7   End session

Compliments I'm really impressed with .... (something linked to the best hopes)
Invitation: to watch out for any signs of progress in moving up the scale
Give: Coaching Card, Sticker, Thank you Card, Scale

Figure 8.14 (continued from page 137)

Certificates

Celebrating progress and change is part of SFBC sessions, and you will often be asking about small successes and celebrating them during your conversations with children and young people. Using credit cards with children and young people also allows them to celebrate their progress themselves during the coaching – and is a way to help them to acknowledge who has been supporting them by giving credit cards to others. Ben Furman included acknowledging and celebrating in his groundbreaking Kids' Skills Programme (Furman 2004), which focuses on children being in charge of learning and developing their skills, rather than experts analysing their problems and prescribing the solutions. Michael White and David Epston provide many inspiring examples of using certificates as 'counter documents' to celebrate the new stories clients create for themselves which can be spread in their communities (White and Epston 1990). The nature of SFBC means that there are often no final or closing sessions. However, on the occasions when I have known that there will be a final session, I make use of certificates, particularly with younger children. Giving certificates can be an opportunity to summarise, to compliment, and to firm up changes made, particularly if it is the child who does the summarising. I have also found that, with some children and young people, working on what they want in small chunks or sections seems more helpful to them, and in these cases a number of certificates can work very well. Certificates, like all materials, work best when they are personalised to each child or young person. In my view there can never be too many!

Example 6: Certificates

These include: a 'Final' certificate (see Figure 8.15) and a 'Personalised' certificate (see Figure 8.16).

Figure 8.15

Figure 8.16

References

Buzan, T. (2005) *The Ultimate Book of Mind Maps*. London: HarperCollins/Thorsons.

Furman, B. (2004) *Kids' Skills, Playful and Practical Solution-Finding With Children*. Australia: St Lukes' Innovative Resources.

Selekman, M.D. (1997) *Solution-Focused Therapy With Children*. New York: Guildford Press.

White, M. and Epston, D. (1990) *Narrative Means to Therapeutic Ends*. New York: W. W. Norton.

Index

'Great Instead, the' 8
groupwork 69–84; and attention span 72,
    73; ending 82–3; example of 82–7; first
    session in 71–2; maintaining interest in
    78; spontaneous 79; themes in 71
GROW model 11

hand puppets 29
homework 4–5, 31, 43, 97, 100

identity questions 4, 38, 98
imaginary-feelings X-ray machine 29
impartiality 95
instances (of success) 3, 5, 8, 21, 44, 67,
    71, 111, 115, 136, 138

'keeping calm' list 99–100
key techniques in 21, 65; and lists 39–40,
    113, 128,131
Kids' Skills Programme 139

language 3, 11–12, 37–8, 114, 119

materials 27–8, 41, 113, 119–40
mentors 14, 49, 101
Milwaukee model 1, 2, 4, 60
mindfulness 31
mind maps 41, 120, 132–4
Miracle Question 1, 2, 3, 5, 35, 64, 119
models 9, 11, 15, 27, 51, 87, 89
'movies of success' 29

non-verbal behaviour 14, 119
'noticing suggestions' 40

Outcome Rating Scales 82

parents 63–7, 72, 85, 86, 87, 104, 110–11
pastoral staff 85, 101
pathways to change 8, 9, 37, 113
peer counselling 86
peer groups 67, 69, 81
peer relationships 86, 87, 90, 93
physical differences 111
preferred futures 1, 3, 5, 6, 7, 19, 21, 22,
    31, 35, 37, 53, 55, 57, 71, 72, 77, 93,
    120, 128, 136, 137

play 27–8
problem-solving approaches 7
'problem talk' 26
progress rating/scales 2, 4, 5, 6, 16, 21,
    32–3, 36–7, 40, 55, 71, 72, 76, 80–2,
    138
psychotherapy 15, 17, 18

'quote cards' 120

reading 75, 97; difficulties with 85
resource talk 5, 32, 42, 93–4
risk assessment 25, 56, 89
risk-taking 41, 56, 89, 112–13, 117
role play 27, 30, 44, 79, 106

safety issues 18–19, 25, 34, 89
scales 2, 4–6, 16, 21–2, 28, 31, 33, 36–7,
    40, 42–4, 54, 55, 57–60, 76, 78, 80–2,
    102, 105–6, 125–8; commitment 33,
    37, 65; confidence 37, 55, 65;
    coping 37; effort 37; 'jumping' 125;
    other-person perspective 37
scaling questions 32–3, 36, 37, 41, 75, 76,
    78, 80–1
schools setting 85–107
self-harm 19, 57, 89
self-soothing 57
Session Rating Scales 82
sexuality 47
'SF walks' 30–1, 120
significant others 9–10, 21, 48–51, 67, 81,
    98
signs of progress 3–7, 9–10, 21, 22, 31,
    35, 36, 37, 41, 44, 55, 56, 66, 72–5, 81,
    103, 113, 115, 120, 136, 138
Skype 14
social constructionism 11–12
solution behaviour 2
solution development 1
solution focused schools 96
solutions 1, 6, 25, 95, 139
'solution talk' 11
staff meetings 85, 102–3
stories 31, 80, 82, 113, 139; negative 98
strength cards 27, 31, 98, 120–1
strengths/skills 31, 120–1